Our
Spiritual
Lifeline

the
oxygen
of
Christian
prayer

Jim McManus C.Ss.R.

Published by **Redemptorist Publications**
Alphonsus House, Chawton, Hampshire, GU34 3HQ, UK
Tel. +44 (0)1420 88222, Fax +44 (0)1420 88805
Email rp@rpbooks.co.uk, www.rpbooks.co.uk

A registered charity limited by guarantee
Registered in England 3261721

Copyright © Redemptorist Publications 2017
First published May 2017

Text by Jim McManus C.Ss.R.
Edited by Mandy Woods
Designed by Christine Towner

ISBN 978-0-85231-484-5

A CIP catalogue record for this book is available from the British Library

The publisher gratefully acknowledges permission to use the following copyright material:
Excerpts from THE JERUSALEM BIBLE, copyright © 1974, 1989 by Darton, Longman & Todd, Ltd and Doubleday, a division of Random House, Inc. Reprinted by permission.

Printed by Lithgo Press Ltd, Leicester LE8 6NU

I gratefully dedicate this book to the memory
of my deceased parents, who first taught me my prayers,
and also to the memory of my many Redemptorist confrères
whose lives of prayerfulness have been an abiding inspiration
and great encouragement to me in the past sixty years.

— Contents —

❖

— Preface —

St Luke tells us that Jesus told his disciples a parable about the effectiveness of prayer to help them "never lose heart" (Luke 18:1). We all need encouragement to persevere with our daily prayers or to resume the practice of having a dedicated time for our daily prayer.

The aim of this book is to help you to look again at the lifeline of prayer in your own life. We will reflect on how Jesus prayed in his life and on how he taught us to pray, giving us the gift of the Lord's Prayer. As we consider in detail some of our traditional prayers, like the Hail Mary or the Prayer for the Holy Spirit, we will rediscover their freshness and vitality.

We will then be able to look more serenely at the challenges we all face in our times of prayer, such as the temptation to give up, the constant distractions of our thoughts, and even the boredom we often experience during our times of prayer.

You will reflect on your own experience of how, as you go about your daily work, you often find yourself in an inner conversation with the Lord, speaking to him spontaneously in your heart. That is the real gift of prayer, the prayer of the heart. As you read this book you will be invited to develop this private, personal dialogue in your heart with the Lord in ways that suit you yourself.

Jesus calls us his "friends". Each of us has his or her unique way of talking with a friend. You have your own word of friendship for your inner dialogue with the Lord. The Holy Spirit gives you that word and you can pray it with great confidence. This book will help you to reflect more deeply not only on the formal prayers that you say daily, but also on that prayer of your heart, your secret dialogue of love and friendship with Christ.

— Introduction —

In the midst of a storm in our life we all need the security of a lifeline that keeps us from aimlessly drifting with the swirling tide. These storms can blow up quite suddenly and without warning. In the midst of one of these storms we cry out for help. Deep down, we know that even though it may seem we are all alone, that is never really the case, as there is someone out there to whom we can shout for help. Is this voice telling us that the little child within us is crying out for his or her mother in a time of danger? Or is it our very humanity that, in the moment of danger, recognises that somehow we all belong together as human beings and we can turn to one another for help? Or is that sense of somebody to whom we can turn in our time of need the very presence of God within us?

In this book I want to explore how this presence of God within us is the spiritual lifeline that God has placed securely in our hearts. We are clinging to that lifeline of prayer when we call out for help. Listen to the cry of the psalmist:

> Rescue me, Lord, for your faithful love is generous;
> In your tenderness turn towards me;
> do not turn away from your servant,
> be quick and answer me, for I am in trouble.
> Come to my side, redeem me,
> ransom me because of my enemies. (Psalm 69:16-18)

Of course, it is not only in times of trouble, in the midst of some storm, that the inner voice cries out. That same voice shouts out its joy in gratitude when the heart is touched by the goodness, the blessedness of life. Listen to this song of the psalmist:

> Cry out with joy to the Lord, all the earth.
> Serve the Lord with gladness.
> Come before him, singing for joy.
> Know that he, the Lord, is God.
> He made us, we belong to him,
> we are his people, the sheep of his flock.
> (Psalm 100:1-3)

In times of trouble and danger and in times of joy and celebration we want to raise our voices in cries for help or in songs of joy, gratitude and appreciation. Our hearts experience happiness and sorrow, successes and failures, moments of elation and moments of depression. We have a lifeline that enables us to give voice to all these changing moods. We call that lifeline *prayer*, God's great gift to us. It is Jesus Christ our saviour and brother who teaches us how to pray and who fills us with the Holy Spirit so that we can confidently lift up our hearts and minds to God our Father and feel accepted and secure in his presence. Our lifeline becomes engaged.

The psalms are the wonderful prayers of the Church that express every human emotion as we turn to God in sadness or joy, in hope or fear. In the fourth century, St Ambrose, writing about the psalms, said: "The book of psalms is medicine for our spiritual health. Whoever reads it will find in it a medicine to cure the wounds caused by his own particular passions."[1]

"Medicine for our spiritual health"! We need that medicine. Speaking of the psalms, Pope Benedict XVI said: "The Psalms are words that the Holy Spirit has given to us: they are God's Spirit become word."[2]

"God's Spirit become word"! What a beautiful and inspiring description of the psalms. When we are praying the psalms, God's Spirit is with every word we say. Those who pray the psalms each day in the Divine Office of the Church have a great resource for their spiritual health. But other forms of prayer will also provide the spiritual medicine and consolation that we need in life. We will explore these prayers in this book.

The Consolation of Prayer

St Alphonsus de Liguori, writing about the consolation of prayer in his own life, wrote:

> And for myself, I speak the truth, I never feel greater consolation, or greater confidence of my salvation, than when I am praying to God, and recommending myself to him. And I think that the same things happen to other believers; for the other signs of our salvation are uncertain and unstable; but that God hears the person who prays to him with confidence is an infallible truth, as it is infallible that God cannot fail in his promises.[3]

St Alphonsus founded the Redemptorist Congregation in 1732 to preach the Gospel of God's great love and mercy to everyone, especially to those who were poor, marginalised and isolated. He believed that everyone, no matter what their state of life, receives from God the gift of prayer in order for them to become a saint. He wanted to make people aware of the immense treasure they have in prayer each time they spend some precious minutes with their heavenly Father. He encouraged us never to allow our weaknesses or sinfulness to prevent us from confidently coming into the presence of God our Father in prayer because we never come alone. We always come with Jesus our Saviour. As scripture encourages us:

> Since in Jesus, the Son of God we have the supreme high priest who has gone through to the highest heaven, we must never let go of the faith that we have professed. For it is not as if we had a high priest who is incapable of feeling our weaknesses with us; but we have one who was tempted in every way that we are, though he is without sin. Let us be confident, then, in approaching the throne of grace, that

we shall have mercy from him and find grace when we are in need of help. (Hebrews 4:14-16)

Every time we pray we are at the throne of grace and mercy. In the words of St Alphonsus, "The throne of grace is Jesus Christ, who is sitting on the right hand of the Father."[4]

In this book we will explore again the immense riches we have in the familiar prayers that we say each day, such as the Our Father and the Hail Mary. But first of all we will spend time looking at how Jesus prayed to the Father while he was on earth. It is his example of prayer that inspires us to come with him and through him into the presence of God our Father.

Some of us can gratefully acknowledge that our best teachers of prayer were our family members, our parents and often our grandparents, as we grew up. Others discover prayer later on in life. It is my hope that as parents or those about to become parents read this book they will take heart and teach their children by word and example how to pray. That will be their best gift to their children and it will last a lifetime.

In 2017 I celebrated my Diamond Jubilee of Profession as a Redemptorist, and I am very aware that in the past sixty years I have had the support and encouragement of great priests and brothers, men of deep prayer, in every community I lived in. Many of them have since gone to their eternal reward in heaven.

I wish to thank my confrère Fr Peter Morris, who read through the manuscript of this book and made many very helpful recommendations. Sincere thanks also to the editors at Redemptorist Publications for publishing this book.

Fr Jim McManus C.Ss.R.

Chapter 1

Jesus at Prayer

Jesus said to his first disciples, and he says to us, "Learn from me" (Matthew 11:29). Jesus is our teacher. He teaches by his example more than by his words. His first disciples observed how he lived, what he did, and then listened to his teaching. Before he taught them anything about prayer they had observed him closely as he prayed. They became very aware that prayer was his lifeline and they began to feel a hunger to be able to pray just as he was praying. Eventually they asked him: "Lord, teach us to pray, as John taught his disciples" (Luke 11:1). In this chapter, before we discuss our own lifeline of prayer, we will observe Jesus as he prays and then we will consider in detail how Jesus teaches us to pray.

During his boyhood years Jesus would have imitated the prayers that he heard his mother saying. She would have taught him the prayers of the psalms and he would have recited these with his mother and foster father, St Joseph, at their family prayer. He got a good grounding in prayer during those "hidden years" at home in Nazareth. As the Catechism says, "The Son of God who became the Son of the Virgin learned to pray in his human heart. He learns to pray from his mother, who kept all the great things the Almighty had done and treasured them in her heart."[5]

When Jesus begins his public life of preaching the Gospel we frequently see him at prayer. Sometimes, we are told, he spent a whole night in prayer. This made a deep and lasting impression on his disciples. What was he saying to God? How was he praying? They wanted to be able to pray in the way he was praying. Eventually they asked him. We read in Luke's Gospel: "Now it happened that he was in a certain place praying, and when he had finished, one of his disciples asked him, 'Lord, teach us to pray, as John taught his disciples'" (Luke 11:1).

Christ's first disciples were Jews who would have prayed at least three times during the day: in the morning, at midday and in the evening. On Saturdays, they would have been nourished on the scriptures and would have joined in the prayers as the Sabbath liturgy was celebrated each week in the synagogue. They would have been familiar with the prayers of the psalms and with many of the other wonderful prayers that we find throughout the Hebrew scriptures. Yet, they were looking for more. As they observed Jesus at his time of prayer they began to long to pray as he was praying. They knew that prayer was his lifeline with God. But what was he saying to God in his prayers? They also knew that John the Baptist, who had baptised Jesus in the Jordan River, had taught his disciples to pray. If the Baptist's disciples were saying, "John the Baptist taught us how to pray," they wanted to be able to say, "Jesus of Nazareth taught us how to pray." Why was Jesus not teaching them? Like any good teacher, he was waiting until they were ready to receive what he had to teach them.

The Baptism of Jesus

Jesus didn't begin preaching the Gospel until he was about thirty years old. He wasn't in a hurry. St Luke puts it this way: "When he began, Jesus was about thirty years old, being the son, as it was thought, of Joseph" (Luke 3:23). He had lived a quiet, unremarkable life in Nazareth, at home with his mother, Mary, and his foster father, Joseph the carpenter, and surrounded by his first cousins. We know the names of some of them. When Jesus began preaching in Nazareth, his townsfolk were very surprised and said:

> "Where did the man get all this wisdom and these miraculous powers? This is the carpenter's son surely? Is not his mother the woman called Mary, and his brothers James and Joseph and Simon and Jude? His sisters, too, are they not here with us? So where did the man get it all?" And they would not accept him. (Matthew 13:54-57)

Those neighbours in Nazareth thought they knew all about Jesus: about his family; about his trade as a carpenter; about his lack of any formal education. But despite their refusal to accept him, they were asking the right question: "where did the man get all this wisdom and these miraculous powers?"

St Luke could have answered their questions had they been willing to listen. Luke begins his account of Jesus' preaching the Gospel with the account of his baptism in the Jordan River by John the Baptist. This is how he records it:

> Now it happened that when all the people had been baptised and while Jesus after his own baptism was at prayer, heaven opened and the Holy Spirit descended on him in a physical form like a dove. And a voice came from heaven, "You are my Son; today I have fathered you." (Luke 3:21-22)

The baptism of Jesus was the occasion when the God the Father acknowledged him as "his Son" and the Holy Spirit came down and rested on him. We notice that Jesus was at prayer while this manifestation of the Holy Trinity took place. It wasn't through the baptism of John. John, in fact, began to protest when Jesus presented himself for baptism.

When the Baptist first saw Jesus by the Jordan River he said to his disciples, "There is the Lamb of God who takes away the sins of the world. This is the one I spoke of when I said: A man is coming after me who ranks before me because he existed before me" (John 1:30). John believed that Jesus was the Christ, the promised Messiah. We can understand, therefore, that when Jesus presented himself to John for his baptism of repentance, the Baptist hesitated and said, "I should be baptised by you and do you come to me?" (Matthew 3:14). Jesus didn't need his baptism of repentance. But what John didn't fully realise was that in seeking this baptism, Jesus was identifying himself completely with all sinners. As Pope Benedict XVI explained, "Jesus loaded the burdens of mankind's guilt upon his shoulders; he bore it down into the depths of the Jordan. He inaugurated his public activity by stepping into the place of sinners."[6]

Jesus takes our place in his baptism by John and now stands before God, totally identified with all sinners, whose sins he came to take away. God the Father responds to Jesus while he is at prayer. We are not told what Jesus was praying to the Father about. But we can surmise that as he took our place in his baptism at the hands of John, he was asking the Father to fulfil his great promise as related by the prophet Joel: "I will pour out my spirit on all humanity" (Joel 3:1). Or he could have been praying, "You send forth your spirit, they are created; and you renew the face of the earth" (Psalm 104:30). The coming of the Spirit on Jesus, after his baptism, in answer to his prayer, manifests the beginning of our salvation.

On this first occasion, then, when we see Jesus at prayer, that wonderful outpouring of the spirit "on all humanity" takes place in the very humanity of Jesus. Now St Luke can tell us, "Filled with the Holy Spirit, Jesus left the Jordan and was led by the Spirit into the desert, for forty days being put to the test by the devil" (Luke 4:1-2). After his forty days' fast he was ready for his mission. In the words of the evangelist, "Jesus, with the power of the Spirit in him, returned to Galilee and his reputation spread throughout the countryside" (Luke 4:14).

The Choice of the Twelve Apostles

Just as Jesus began his public ministry with prayer to the Father after his baptism, so before he made his big choice of the Twelve he spent the whole night in prayer. This is how St Luke records this great moment:

> Now it happened in those days that he went onto the mountain to pray and he spent the whole night in prayer to God. When day came he summoned his disciples and picked out twelve of them; he called them "apostles":

15

> Simon whom he called Peter, and his brother Andrew, James, Judas, Philip, Bartholomew, Matthew, Thomas, James son of Alphaeus, Simon called the Zealot, Judas son of James, and Judas Iscariot who became a traitor. (Luke 6:12-16)

All night long Jesus was in communion with his heavenly Father as he was preparing to choose the Twelve Apostles.

Peter's Confession of Faith

It was while Jesus was praying that Simon Peter made his great act of faith, professing that Jesus is the Christ of God. St Luke writes:

> Now it happened that he was praying alone, and his disciples came to him and he put this question to them, "Who do the crowds say I am?" And they answered, "Some say John the Baptist; others Elijah; others again one of the ancient prophets come back to life." "But you," he said to them, "who do you say I am?" It was Peter who spoke up. "The Christ of God," he said. (Luke 9:18-20)

We can visualise that particular scene. Jesus was praying alone, showing through his whole being that he was totally immersed in the presence of God his Father. The disciples, knowing what the people were saying about him, and the high esteem in which they held him, were probably observing him praying for some time before they eventually came into his presence. Knowing their thoughts, he asked them: "Who do the crowds say I am?" They were able to tell him that the crowds had a very high opinion of him, and that they were convinced that he was one of the great prophets. But Jesus wanted to know what they thought themselves. And Peter was able to make his great profession of faith: "You are the Christ, the Son of the living God" (Matthew 16:16). How did Peter get that insight? Jesus made it very clear to him and he said:

Simon son of Jonah, you are a blessed man! Because it was no human agency revealed this to you but my Father in heaven. So I now say to you: You are Peter and on this rock I will build my community. And the gates of hell will not overpower it. I will give you the keys of the kingdom of Heaven; whatever you bind on earth will be bound in heaven; whatever you loose on earth will be loosed in heaven. (Matthew 16:17-19)

Peter's profession of faith in Christ arose in the context of his attentive observing of Jesus at prayer. And from his deep prayer with his Father, Jesus reciprocated with his own profession of faith in Peter, proclaiming that he was the rock on which his Church would be built.

Jesus' Prayer of Joy

Jesus not only taught his disciples the good news that he came to bring to the human race but he also sent them out to proclaim it. It was as if he said to them, "You have heard what I have been teaching you, now you go and teach others." St Luke tells us: "After this the Lord appointed seventy-two others and sent them out ahead of him in pairs, to all the towns and places he himself would be visiting. And he said to them, 'The harvest is rich but the labourers are few, so ask the Lord of the harvest to send labourers into his harvesting'" (Luke 10:1-2). Those disciples set off on their first missionary journey and they began to experience for themselves the power of preaching in the name of Jesus. They had great reports for Jesus on their return. St Luke says, "The seventy-two came back rejoicing. 'Lord,' they said, 'even the devils submit to us when we use your name'" (Luke 10:17). They had been witnessing to Christ and they experienced that by using the very name "Jesus", Christ himself had been with them. As Pope Benedict XVI said, "We become witnesses when, through our actions, words and way of being, Another makes himself present."[7] Jesus was present in their preaching. That is why the devils submitted to them. But Jesus said to them, "Do not rejoice that the spirits submit to you; rejoice instead that your names are written in heaven" (Luke 10:20).

Jesus himself was filled with joy as those disciples came back to him and reported all their experience of preaching in his name. St Luke writes:

> Jesus at this time, filled with joy by the Holy Spirit said, "I bless you, Father, Lord of heaven and earth, for hiding these things from the learned and the clever and revealing them to little children. Yes, Father, for that it is what it pleased you to do. Everything has been entrusted to me by my Father; and no one knows who the Son is except the Father, and who the Father is except the Son and those to whom the Son chooses to reveal him." (Luke 10:21-22)

We can hear the joy of Jesus in that prayer of blessing, acknowledging that the Father was indeed revealing the great mystery of our salvation to "little children". He had, of course, warned us: "In truth I tell you, unless you change and become like little children, you will never enter the kingdom of God" (Matthew 18:3). Now his disciples were entering the kingdom of God because, like little children, they were putting all their trust in him. That was the source of their joy and the source of Jesus' joy, the joy of the Gospel. As Pope Francis wrote, "The joy of the Gospel fills the hearts and lives of all who encounter Jesus. Those who accept his offer of salvation are set free from sin, sorrow, inner emptiness and loneliness."[8] When we experience that joy of the Gospel we respond in prayer as Jesus did and say, "We bless you Father, Lord of heaven and of earth, for hiding these things from the learned and the clever and for revealing them to little children" – that is, for revealing them to us today.

The Transfiguration

While Jesus was at prayer on the mountain, Peter, James and John witnessed a visible manifestation of the truth about Jesus that Peter had professed – namely, that he was the "the Christ, the Son of the living God". St Luke describes it in this way:

> Now about eight days after this had been said, he took Peter, John and James and went up a mountain to pray. And it happened that, as he was praying, the aspect of his face was changed and his clothing became sparkling white. And suddenly there were two men talking to him; they were Moses and Elijah appearing in glory, and they were speaking of his passing which he was to accomplish in Jerusalem... A cloud came and covered them with its shadow; and when they went into the cloud the disciples were afraid. And a voice came from the cloud saying, "This is my Son, the Chosen One. Listen to him." (Luke 9:28-35)

The transfiguration of Jesus on the mountain is a prayer event. This great manifestation of the glory of Christ takes place as Jesus is in communion with his Father. Moses and Elijah come to talk to Jesus "about his passing which he was to accomplish in Jerusalem". "His passing" literally means "his Exodus", which connects Jesus' approaching passion and death with that first Exodus of God's people when Moses, who is now talking to Jesus on the mountain, led them from slavery in Egypt into freedom. The death of Jesus will be the "second Exodus" of God's people, not into an earthly kingdom, but into the kingdom of God. The salvation symbolised by the first Exodus is about to be realised in Jesus' Exodus from this world to the glory of the Father. Moses and the great prophet Elijah are talking to Jesus about his approaching passion and death. Pope Benedict XVI wrote:

Their topic of conversation is the Cross, but understood in the inclusive sense of Jesus' Exodus, which had to take place in Jerusalem. Jesus' Cross is an Exodus: a departure from this life, a passage through the "Red Sea" of the Passion and a transition into glory – glory, however, that forever bears the mark of Jesus' wounds.[9]

Witnessing the transfiguration of Jesus on the mountain was a most profound experience for the three disciples. It is first and foremost an experience of what happens when Jesus prays. Because this mystery of the transfiguration is an experience of Jesus at prayer, it can become for us also a great "prayer event" as we behold in our meditation the glory of God shining on the face of Jesus. Peter could never forget it. In his second letter to the churches he wrote, "He was honoured and glorified by God the Father, when a voice came to him from the transcendent Glory: *This is my Son, the Beloved; he enjoys my favour.* We ourselves heard this voice from heaven, when we were with him on the holy mountain" (2 Peter 1:17-18).

Jesus Teaches His Disciples the Lord's Prayer

The disciples were observing Jesus as he went around preaching the Gospel, healing the sick and casting out evil spirits. They became aware that he did nothing without first praying about it. And they were also conscious that he had said nothing to them about prayer or how they should be praying. Eventually one of them asked him to teach them. St Luke tells us: "Now it happened that he was in a certain place praying, and when he had finished, one of his disciples said, 'Lord, teach us to pray, as John taught his disciples.' He said to them, 'When you pray, this is what to say: *Father, may your name be held holy*'" (Luke 11:1-2). Jesus taught his enquiring disciples the most amazing word to speak to God in prayer. He told them that the very first word they should use when they turned to God in prayer is *Father – our Father.* That is a revelation, an extraordinary truth that Jesus is making known to them. God is not the distant great architect of the universe. He is our loving Father. The disciples were now getting their first glimpse into how Jesus was praying. He was in the presence of his Father and he was having a loving conversation with his Father. That is how Jesus wanted them to pray. That is how Jesus wants us to pray. We too, when we pray, are in the presence of our Father. Like Jesus, we too can have a loving conversation with our God. Pope Benedict XVI commented:

> The fact that Luke places the Our Father in the context of Jesus' own praying is therefore significant. Jesus thereby involves us in his own prayer; he leads us into the interior dialogue of triune love; he draws our human hardships deep into God's heart.[10]

We are very familiar with the Lord's Prayer. In the third chapter of this book we will reflect in detail on how Jesus teaches us profound truths in this prayer, not only about God, but also about ourselves. The Lord's Prayer is a formation of both mind and heart. By teaching us to say "Our Father" (Matthew 6:9)[11] in our prayer to God, Jesus is revealing to us that our relationship with God is defined by that word *our*. Who do we include when we say *our Father*?

Jesus' Great Prayer for His Disciples

At the Last Supper, after he had washed the feet of his disciples, Jesus offered a wonderful and most encouraging prayer to God his Father for his disciples. This prayer is called *The High Priestly Prayer* and we find it in chapter 17 of John's Gospel. There we read:

> Father, the hour has come:
> glorify your Son
> so that your Son may glorify you;
> so that, just as you have given him
> power over all humanity,
> he may give eternal life
> to all those you have entrusted to him

And eternal life is this:
to know you,
the only true God
and Jesus Christ whom you have sent. (John 17:1-3)

Jesus, whom we have often seen praying alone, with the disciples observing him, now prays in their midst and prays specifically for them. He prays that the Father will glorify him so that he will give eternal life to all his disciples. And he gives us this definition of eternal life: "to know you the only true God and Jesus Christ whom you have sent" (John 17:3). Notice, he is not praying that we have life after death. He is praying that we have eternal life in the present. That eternal life consists in knowing the one true God and in knowing Jesus Christ. This is not abstract knowledge. This is a knowledge that leads to communion, to a loving relationship with God our Father and with Our Lord Jesus Christ which gives a whole new meaning and purpose to life. That is what we mean by our Christian faith. As Pope Benedict XVI wrote: "Being a Christian is not the result of an ethical choice or a lofty idea, but an encounter with an event, a person which gives life a new horizon and a definitive direction."[12]

Jesus prayed that we would have this encounter with him, that we would have this personal knowledge of him, because he wants, as he said, to "share [his] joy with [us] to the full" (John 17:13). On the night before he suffered the agony of his death on the cross, Jesus prayed to God the Father for you and me, prayed that we would have eternal life, true life, in this world and participate fully in his joy.

Those who pray always wish good things for others. Jesus prayed throughout his life, and now he wishes the most wonderful thing for us: communion with the Father, friendship with himself and true life, abundant life, as we live as his disciples in this world. And at the end of our life in this world, he will fulfil his great promise to us: "Anyone who does eat my flesh and drink my blood has eternal life and I will raise that person up on the last day" (John 6:56).

Jesus promises us that he will raise us up to a new life, the life of the resurrection which he himself now lives with the Father and the Holy Spirit, after our death in this world. His great prayer for us, the wonderful promise he makes to us, is the source of our joy and hope in this world.

May They All Be One

In his great High Priestly Prayer at his Last Supper, Jesus prayed, not just for the disciples gathered around the table with him, but for everyone who would believe in him through their preaching. The request Jesus made to his Father shows us what was uppermost in his mind and heart at that moment. This is how he prayed: "I pray not only for these but also for those who through their teaching will come to believe in me. May they all be one, just as, Father, you are in me and I am in you, so that they also may be in us, so that the world may believe it was you who sent me" (John 17:20-21).

This unity among all his future disciples down through the ages was so important for Jesus that during his long High Priestly Prayer he prayed four times for it: "Holy Father, keep those you have given me true to your name, so that they may be one like us" (John 17:11); "May they all be one, just as Father, you are in me and I am in you" (John 17:21); "I have given them the glory you gave to me, that they may be one as we are one" (John 17:22); "With me in them and you in me, may they be so perfected in unity that the world will recognise that it was you who sent me and that you have loved them as you have loved me" (John 17:23).

Jesus identifies the source of the unity which he wants his disciples to experience. Just as he and God the Father, in the great mystery of the Holy Trinity, are one, so he desires this same unity for all his disciples. Jesus emphasises twice the purpose this unity of his disciples will serve: "That the world may believe it was you who sent me" (John 17:21. 23). Jesus prayed that his followers would be recognised by their unity, by their love for each other, by their eagerness to tell the whole world that the source of their unity can only be found in God. This is why the Second Vatican Council defined the Church in terms of this unity. It teaches: "The Church is a people brought into unity from the unity of the Father, the Son and the Holy Spirit."[13]

The Second Vatican Council recognised that the Lord who prayed so longingly for the unity of all his disciples at the Last Supper was giving special grace to Christians of all denominations in our time to seek unity more seriously. It stated: "Everywhere large numbers have felt the impulse of this grace and among our separated brethren also there increases from day to day a movement, fostered by the grace of the Holy Spirit, for the restoration of unity among all Christians."[14]

The Catholic Church acknowledges that the ecumenical movement is the work of the Holy Spirit who is guiding all Christians to open their hearts to Christ's great prayer for unity among all his disciples. That is why we should frequently listen to these great prayers that Jesus prayed for us.

Jesus' Prayer for Peter

At the Last Supper Jesus singled out Peter for a special prayer. He said to him: "Simon, Simon! Look, Satan has got his wish to sift you all like wheat; but I have prayed for you, Simon, that your faith may not fail, and once you have recovered, you in your turn must strengthen your brothers" (Luke 22:31-32). Why did Jesus single Peter out for this special prayer? Because Peter was the rock on which Jesus said he would build his Church. That great prayer of Jesus rests on Peter and all his successors as Bishop of Rome. In response to Jesus' question, "Who do you say I am?", Peter spoke up for the Twelve and said, "You are the Christ, the Son of the living God." Jesus then gave him his new name: "I now say to you; You are Peter and on this rock I will build my Church" (Matthew 16:15-18).

Peter, the rock, was in great need of that special prayer of Jesus when he collapsed through fear in the courtyard as Jesus was being tried before the High Priest, and denied that he ever knew Jesus. St Mark records Peter's collapse:

> While Peter was down below in the courtyard, one of the high priest's servant-girls came up. She saw Peter warming himself there, looked closely at him and said, "You too were with Jesus, the man from Nazareth." But he denied it. "I do not know. I do not understand what you are talking about," he said. And he went out into the forecourt, and a cock crowed. The servant girl saw him again and started telling the bystanders, "This man is one of them." But again he denied it. A little later the bystanders themselves said to Peter, "You are certainly one of them! Why, you are a Galilean." But he started cursing and swearing. "I do not know the man you speak of." And at once the cock crowed for the second time, and Peter recalled what Jesus had said to him, "Before the cock crows twice, you will have disowned me three times." And he burst into tears. (Mark 14:66-72)

The prayer of Jesus for Peter produced that deep sorrow in his heart. He wept for his denial and he trusted in the love and the mercy of Jesus. He recovered from his fall and, as Jesus said, "he strengthened his brothers". Today we are very aware that Pope Francis, the successor of Peter as the Bishop of Rome, continues that Petrine ministry of supporting his brothers and sisters in all their struggles and weaknesses.

Jesus at Prayer during His Agony in the Garden

St Matthew concludes his account of the Last Supper and the gift of the Holy Eucharist with these words: "After the psalms had been sung they left for the Mount of Olives" (Matthew 26:30). Jesus was singing hymns of praise and thanks to God on his way to the garden of Gethsemane. In giving us the gift of the Holy Eucharist, he had offered himself to the Father with the words, "Drink from this all of you, for this is my blood, the blood of the covenant, poured out for many for the forgiveness of sins" (Matthew 26:28). Jesus freely and joyfully offered his whole life for our salvation. But now he realises that his enemies are closing in and that he is facing a cruel death in this world. So after his Last Supper with his disciples, he retreats to the garden where he can spend his last few hours with his heavenly Father in prayer. God's will was that Jesus would bring to all people the good news of our salvation. By faithfully doing that, Jesus incurred the enmity, the rejection and finally the death sentence that sinful humanity passed on him.

Peter, James and John were with Jesus when he was transfigured on the mountain. Now he takes them with him as he withdraws to a distance from the other apostles. He needs their prayerful support because he is now facing his greatest struggle. He said to them, "My soul is sorrowful to the point of death. Wait here and stay awake with me" (Matthew 26:38). Jesus knew that "his hour" had come. At the beginning of the Last Supper he had prayed: "Father, the hour has come: glorify your Son so that your Son may glorify you" (John 17:1). Because of our human sinfulness that glorification will now have to take place on the cross. Jesus had foretold it: "When I am lifted up from the earth, I shall draw all people to myself." And John adds, "By these words he indicated the kind of death he would die" (John 12:32-33). Jesus knew that he had to face a time of horrendous suffering, pain and death, and that dreadful awareness filled his whole being with anguish and terror. He fell on his face and cried out to his Father, "If you are willing, take this cup away from me. Nevertheless, let your will be done, not mine" (Luke 22:42).

His agony was real. St Luke says, "In his anguish he prayed even more earnestly, and his sweat fell to the grounds like drops of blood" (Luke 22:44). Jesus was not like the false pagan gods who could not be touched by human suffering. Jesus, in being born into this world, as St Paul says, "emptied himself, taking the form of a slave, becoming as human beings are" (Philippians 2:7). In his humanity, our humanity, Jesus feels all the anguish and terror of his approaching passion. In his baptism in the Jordan River by John the Baptist, Jesus identified himself totally with our sinful humanity. Now in the Garden of Gethsemane, mankind's guilt is bearing down heavily upon him. He falls prostrate on the ground and prays, "Abba, Father, for you everything is possible. Take this cup from me. But let it be as you, not I, would have it" (Mark 14:36). He is one with the Father and God the Father is one with him and together they are involved in the work of our redemption. He had made this clear when he said to Nicodemus, "Yes, God loved the world so much that he gave his only Son, so that everyone who believes in him may not be lost but may have eternal life. For God sent his Son into the world not to condemn the world, but so that through him the world might be saved" (John 3:16-17).

During Jesus' transfiguration on the mountain, Moses and Elijah talked with him about "the Exodus" that he would accomplish in Jerusalem (Luke 9:31), the "new Exodus" when he would lead God's people into the kingdom of God. Now his hour has come and he submits his human will to God's will. He says the prayer that his mother said when she consented to become his mother: "Let it happen to me as you have said" (Luke 1:38). Many times during his preaching Jesus said, "I have come from heaven, not to do my own will, but to do the will of the one who sent me" (John 6:38).

The will of the Father is for Jesus to lead us in the "new Exodus" into the kingdom of God. But Jesus' enemies, and especially the evil one, Satan, are determined to destroy him, by having him condemned to the horrible death by crucifixion. Facing this time of horrendous suffering, Jesus prayed to the Father "your will be done", and an angel came "and gave him strength" (Luke 22:42-43). St John concludes his account of the agony in Gethsemane with these words:

"Knowing everything that was to happen to him, Jesus then came forward and said [to those who had come to arrest him] 'Who are you looking for?' They answered, 'Jesus the Nazarene.' He said, 'I am he.'… When Jesus said, 'I am he', they moved back and fell to the ground" (John 18:4-6). After his agony Jesus faces his captors with serenity and dignity. They are the ones who fall to the ground as he proclaims "I am he." But he allows them to take him prisoner.

Jesus' Final Prayer on the Cross

St Luke records the final prayer that Jesus offered just before he died on the cross. He said his great prayer of forgiveness: "Father, forgive them; they do not know what they are doing" (Luke 23:34). His thoughts were for his enemies, for those who had plotted and planned his death. He knew that even though they thought that they were upholding the law of Moses, they were acting in sheer ignorance. And so he pleaded with his Father for their forgiveness. And then, St Luke tells us, "Jesus cried out in a loud voice saying, 'Father, into your hands I commit my spirit.' With these words he breathed his last" (Luke 23:46).

Speaking about his approaching death, Jesus said to his disciples: "The Father loves me, because I lay down my life in order to take it up again. No one takes it from me; I lay it down of my own free will, and as I have the power to lay it down, so I have the power to take it up again; and this is the command I have received from my Father" (John 10:17-18). Jesus' final act in this world was his prayer to the Father as he said, "Father, into your hands I commit my spirit." His act of dying was his final prayer to his Father. We are told, "Christ offered himself, blameless as he was, to God through the eternal Spirit" (Hebrews 9:14). Notice that it was through the "eternal Spirit", the Holy Spirit, that Jesus offered his life to God on the cross for our salvation. He died through the power of the Holy Spirit just as he was conceived in his Mother's womb through the power of the Holy Spirit. It was through the Holy Spirit that he said his final prayer: "Father, into your hands I commit my spirit."

Jesus wants his final prayer, the prayer he said as he was dying, to be our final prayer as we are about to leave this world. In learning to pray during our life, as Jesus prayed during his life, we too will say as we are about to die, "Father, into your hands I commit my spirit." This is the nightly prayer of the Church in the Divine Office:

> Into your hands, Lord, I commend my spirit. You have redeemed us, Lord God of truth – Into your hands, Lord, I commend my spirit. Glory be to the Father and to the Son and to the Holy Spirit – Into your hands, Lord, I commend my spirit.

As we make this confident commitment of our whole life to God our Father, we can leave all our worries in his hands as we go to sleep.

Chapter 2

Preparing Our Heart and Mind for Prayer

Every time we see Jesus at prayer, something important is about to happen. This should inspire us to prepare ourselves well for our times of prayer. When we begin to pray, three very important questions are at the back of our minds, though we may not always be aware of them. First of all, we ask ourselves where we are at the very moment of crossing the threshold of prayer. Second, we ask ourselves who we are with as we cross the threshold of prayer. And third, most important of all, we ask ourselves what right we have to come into God's presence and demand his attention.

On Holy Ground

When we cross the threshold of prayer we are consciously seeking to enter into the presence of God. That threshold is not in some holy place far away and outside ourselves but within our own hearts. Sometimes, like St Augustine, we may seek God outside ourselves to no avail. He wrote: "You were within and I was outside."[15] God is closer to us than we are to ourselves. When Moses approached the burning bush he was told, "Take off your sandals because the place where you are standing is holy ground" (Exodus 3:5). We are on holy ground when we enter the presence of God. We do so with reverence.

We need an interior preparation of mind and heart as we begin all our prayers. In your living room or in your bedroom, as you turn to God in prayer, you turn off the TV or the radio, you enter into the presence of God, and your living room or your bedroom becomes holy ground. You become aware that God is with you. Of course, God is with you always, even when you are totally unaware of his presence, but once you become aware of his presence with you, your very surroundings take on a new meaning. You realise that you are on holy ground and that your home has become holy. You can now see your home as the place where God dwells. Now your prayer time at home becomes very significant and very important. Your home becomes the house of God where you and your family and all your friends can be at peace in God's presence, in Christ's presence.

In the Gospels there are many times that we see Christ sitting at table, enjoying a meal with his friends and with those who invited him to be their guest. In a special way in your home, as you lift your mind and heart up to God, Christ joins you at "your table" as your guest. He says, "Look, I am standing at the door, knocking. If one of you hears me calling and opens the door, I will come in to share a meal at that person's side" (Revelation 3:20). A moment of interior reflection will help you to become aware in faith of his presence. Once you begin to realise where you are, that you are now "at table with Christ", you will be ready in heart and mind to have a friendly conversation with the Lord. You will have taken the first necessary step in that act of prayer which we often define as lifting our minds and hearts up to God. You will have done what we say we do when the priest, during Mass, invites us to "lift up your hearts" and we respond with the words "We lift them up to the Lord." When our hearts are lifted up to the Lord we are in a state of prayer. We are now in communion with God, in an intimate, personal union with Father, Son and Holy Spirit.

With the Whole Christ

Another question that we have is this: who am I with as I cross the threshold of prayer? When you come into the presence of God in prayer, even if you are just by yourself, you are never alone. It is never just yourself and God. As Jesus taught us, our first words in prayer are *Our Father*. In God's presence we are always his family. Because we are members of Christ's body on earth, the whole Christ is present when we come before God our Father in prayer. St Paul

31

tells us that "Christ is the Head of the Body that is the Church" (Colossians 1:18). That means that wherever we are, we are there as the members of God's family that we call the Church, which is Christ's body on earth.

Because each of us is a member of Christ's body, we try to keep this in mind when we turn to God in prayer. During the Mass, the Church teaches us to consciously join our voices with the voices of all the angels and saints of God with these words: "And so, with Angels and Archangels, with Thrones and Dominions, and with all the hosts and Powers of heaven, we sing the hymn of your glory." We consciously join our voices with the voices of all the angels in heaven. But not just with those angelic hosts. We also unite our voices with all those who have gone before us and who are now living for ever with God. We join our voices with the most blessed Virgin Mary, the Mother of God, blessed Joseph her spouse, with the blessed Apostles and with all the Saints. At Mass we also remember "our departed brothers and sisters and all who were pleasing to you at their passing from this life" (Eucharistic Prayer 3), and, of course, we remember all our brothers and sisters throughout the world at this present time. In our great prayer at Mass we consciously proclaim that we are united with all the angels and saints in heaven, with all those who have died in God's mercy, and with all our brothers and sisters throughout the world. So we are never alone when we are at our prayer in God's presence.

As members of Christ's body, each one of us represents that body when we come into God's presence to pray. Not only that, the whole body of Christ stands with us as we pray. So, it is not just you, as a single individual, who has come into God's presence. You bring, as it were, the whole Church with you. Because you are in Christ and Christ is our head, then it is Christ himself who is with you every time you come into God the Father's presence. It is in Christ and through Christ that you have access to the Father. In a beautiful sermon, St Augustine put it this way:

God could give no greater gift to men and women than to make his Word, through whom he created all things, their head and to join them to him as his members, so that the Word might be both Son of God and son of man, one God with the Father, and one man with all men and women. The result is that when we speak to God in prayer we do not separate the Son from him, and when the body of the Son prays it does not separate its head from itself: it is one Saviour of his body, one Lord Jesus Christ, the Son of God, who prays for us and in us and is himself the object our prayer. Christ prays for us as our priest, he prays in us as our head, he is the object of our prayers as our God.[16]

Christ Prays for Us as Our Priest

The most consoling truth, especially when we are finding it hard to pray, is that Christ is our High Priest and Redeemer. At the very moment we turn to God the Father in prayer, Christ is interceding for us. Our prayer is our response to Christ's prayer in us. The urge to pray, even to say "a few quick prayers", didn't come from ourselves. It is an invitation from Christ, who is already interceding for us. We read in Hebrews: "His power to save those who come to God through him is absolute, since he lives for ever to intercede for them" (Hebrews 7:25). As Jesus Christ prays for us as our priest and as he prays in us as our head, he exercises his absolute power to save us.

Christ always wants to free us from the fear of approaching God in prayer because of our sinfulness, our weaknesses and our many failures. He sympathises with us in all our weaknesses. As scripture tells us:

> The high priest we have is not incapable of feeling our weaknesses with us, but has been put to the test in exactly the same way as ourselves, apart from sin. Let us, then, have no fear in approaching the throne of grace to receive mercy and to find grace when we are in need of help. (Hebrews 4:15-16)

Christ's high-priestly office in heaven is exercised on earth as he prays for each of us who come into the presence of God in his name. We remind ourselves of this when, during Mass, we often say in our penitential act these words: "You are seated at the right hand of the Father to intercede for us: Lord have mercy." When we ask Christ our Lord for mercy we are opening our lives to enable him to accomplish in us the very goal he had when he became a human being like us. The angel of the Lord said to St Joseph: "Do not be afraid to take Mary home as your wife, because she has conceived what is in her by the Holy Spirit. She will give birth to a son and you must name him Jesus, because he is the one who is to save his people from their sins" (Matthew 1:20-21).

When we pray, "Lord have mercy, Christ have mercy", we are asking Jesus to do for us what he came into this world to do – namely, to be for us the mercy of God and to redeem us from all our sins. We say in the Creed, "For us men and women and for our salvation he came down from heaven and by the Holy Spirit was incarnate of the Blessed Virgin Mary and became man." Christ, then, rejoices when we appeal for his mercy. He told us that "there will be more rejoicing in heaven over one sinner repenting than over ninety-nine upright people who have no need of repentance" (Luke 15:7).

We can now answer the second question, "who are we with as we cross the threshold of prayer?" As members of Christ's body, the Church, we are with the whole Christ. And Christ our Lord is praying in us and for us. We can now unite our prayers with the prayer of the whole Christ. We are never all alone in God's presence. Even our enemies are with us, because they too are members of Christ. They too have a place in that "*our*" which we speak to God when we say *Our Father.* And when we experience all our weaknesses and distractions, instead of concluding that we are no good at praying, we can take comfort from the words of St Paul:

> The Spirit too comes to help us in our weakness, for, when we do not know how to pray properly, then the Spirit personally makes our petitions for us in groans that cannot be put into words; and he who can see into our hearts knows what the Spirit means because the prayers that the Spirit makes for God's holy people are always in accordance with the mind of God. (Romans 8:26-27)

When we do our best to prepare our minds and hearts for our time of prayer with God, by remembering where we are and who we are with, we can then surrender the results of all our efforts to the Holy Spirit and to Christ, who are praying in us. Christ, our high priest, is seated at the right hand of the Father interceding for us and he also prays in us as our priest. His Holy Spirit whom he has given to us to be our encourager, our sanctifier and our comforter also prays in us. Even before we come to our time of prayer we are being well prayed for by Christ, at the right hand of God the Father, and by the Holy Spirit in our hearts. A moment of recollection as we are about to begin our prayer helps us to become aware that these powerful, divine intercessors are already praying for us, even before we begin to pray ourselves. They have taken the initiative. We can then see our prayer as our response to their prayer in us and for us.

What Right Have We to Come into God's Presence and Demand his Attention?

As we sit in God's presence, maybe sometimes wondering what we are doing there, it is both necessary and helpful to remind ourselves that we have an absolute right to be in his presence, because God is our loving Father and we are his sons and daughters. Christ has revealed this wonderful truth to us. He says to us, "You should pray like this: Our Father who art in heaven..." (Matthew 6:9). Entering into God's presence in prayer is our personal acknowledgement of who we are and of who God is: God is our Father, which means we are in truth God's sons and daughters. St Paul summarises the great work of our redemption in this way:

> God sent his Son, born of a woman, born a subject of the Law, to redeem the subjects of the Law, so that we could receive adoption as sons. As you are sons, God has sent into our hearts the Spirit of his Son crying, "*Abba,* Father"; and so you are no longer a slave, but a son, and if a son, then an heir, by God's own act. (Galatians 4:4-7)

Our Surname is God

When we say we are the daughters and sons of God we are identifying our deepest reality, our true identity. Pope Francis highlighted this well when he said: "To say it simply: we bear God's surname. Our surname is God. He is the root of our vocation to holiness."[17] Children normally receive their surname from their fathers. As you come into God's presence in your prayer time, you are acknowledging that God is your Father; you definitely bear his surname; he acknowledges you as his son or daughter and assures you that you have an absolute right to come into his presence. Because we are sinful, Christ not only revealed that God is our Father, he also revealed to us the qualities of our Father: all loving, all merciful, compassionate, forgiving, comforting, consoling, encouraging and many other endearing features that are summed up in this beautiful description by St John: "God is love. God's love for us was revealed when God sent into the world his only Son so that we could have life through him" (1 John 4:8-9).

When we say, "God is love" we have to remind ourselves that God is infinite love, that God loves us unconditionally, and that there is nothing we can do that will ever force God to stop loving us. We experience human love, which is a beautiful and life-giving experience. We are then inclined to conclude that God loves us in the same way. But we have to remind ourselves regularly that the love God has for us is really unimaginable. It can be compared to the love of parents for their children, of spouses for one another, of brothers and sisters, of friends and so on. But, in reality, the love that God has for us remains a mystery. As Wilfrid Harrington reminds us:

> God is Mystery, a Being wholly different from anything we know in our world. The human mind can shape no adequate idea of God. Consequently, no human word about God can be taken literally. We speak of God analogically. The process works like this. One makes an affirmation: God is good. But this must be immediately qualified: God is not good in the manner of creatures. The conclusion: God is the source of all good. But, then, what is the source of all good? In fact, our human understanding of God gives us but an inkling of what it might mean to be the source of goodness. Similarly, our human understanding of love, even the finest, can give us no appreciation of divine love.[18]

Keeping in mind that our experience of human love can give us just an inkling of the love God has for us, we can say that God our heavenly Father, like any human father, takes delight in his children, especially when they come to spend time with him. He tells us what he thinks of us and how he sees us and he invites us to believe every word he says to us about ourselves and to live by his every word. Let us remind ourselves of some of those wonderful, life-giving words that God speaks to us about ourselves.

The very first thing God says to us about ourselves is that we are created in the image and likeness of God (Genesis 1). We are off to a very good start in life! But, as we know from the scriptures and from our own experience, our first parents lost that state of grace with which God had enriched them in their creation. The Bible records the story of how God came to restore to us, "the fallen children of Adam", what we lost through that rupture between God and us. We call that story our salvation history. The Letter to the Hebrews summarises that history in this way:

> At many moments in the past and by many means, God spoke to our ancestors through the prophets; but in our time, the final days, he has spoken to us in the person of his Son, whom he appointed heir of all things and through whom he made the ages. He is the reflection of God's glory and bears the impress of God's own being, sustaining all things by his powerful command; and now that he has purged sins away, he has taken his seat at the right hand of the divine Majesty on high. (Hebrews 1:1-3)

Even before Christ came as our redeemer, God spoke his life-giving words to his people, assuring them of his presence, his care and his protection. He reminded them, in the words of the psalmist, that they "were created little less than a god and crowned with glory and beauty" (Psalm 8:5). He told them through his prophets that they "were precious in his sight and that he loved them and gave them honour" (Isaiah 43:4). He said, "I shall not forget you. Look, I have engraved you on the palms of my hands" (Isaiah 49:15-16).

Christ Has United Himself with Each Human Being

In a wonderful teaching the Second Vatican Council said: "By his incarnation the Son of God has in a certain way united himself with each individual."[19] This means that every single human being ever born into this world has Jesus Christ as a brother. That is the mystery of God becoming man, God becoming a member of the human race. The Second Vatican Council taught this very consoling doctrine: "Since Christ died for everyone, and since all are called to one and the same destiny, which is divine, we must hold that the Holy Spirit offers to all the possibility of being made partners, in a way known to God, in the paschal mystery."[20]

The mystery of God's infinite love for each human being ever born into this world is beyond our comprehension. Not everyone shares our Christian faith, but we believe that God gives to each person ever born into this world the equal opportunity of receiving eternal life. As St Paul wrote, "God wants everyone to be saved and reach full knowledge of the truth" (1 Timothy 2:3-4). And writing to the Romans, St Paul said, "God has no favourites" (Romans 2:11). Christians are not God's favourites. God has given us the light of faith, and in that faith we believe that we are God's sons and daughters. That is why we have the right to come into God's presence, speak to him in prayer, ask him for all that we need and pray for the whole human race. God loves equally those who, as yet, do not believe in Christ and those who do accept Jesus as their Lord and Saviour.

Jesus said, "Everything has been entrusted to me by my Father; and no one knows the Son except the Father, just as no one knows the Father except the Son and those to whom the Son chooses to reveal him" (Matthew 11:27). The very fact that we believe in God our Father means that Jesus has given us that revelation in our hearts. He has given us the light of faith. It is in and through that light of faith that we find our way into the presence of God in prayer. In God's presence, then, we know who we are – we are the sons and daughters of God our Father who takes delight in us. We have come "to the throne of grace to receive mercy and to find grace when we are in need of help" (Hebrews 4:16). We will not leave God's presence empty-handed.

Our Prayer Time

God has given us the gift of prayer as our lifeline with him. Because it is our lifeline it should always be accorded priority time. We have many fixed times for doing our various tasks during the day: our time for getting up and for going to bed; our time for getting the kids out to school and for being at home when they come back; our time for breakfast, lunch and the evening meal; our time for going to work and for coming back from work; our time for relaxation, for watching TV, for reading a book or for listening to music or the radio; and those times when the family needs our full attention. And somewhere in this busy timetable, we have time to pray.

Where do you schedule your prayer time? What priority does it have in your daily timetable? Experience teaches most people that if prayer is not the top priority in one's day it will take second place to every other good work that has to be done. If my prayer time is not my top priority then I may find myself saying, *I will pray when I have the time* or *I will pray when I feel like it.* If I plan my prayer life along those lines I will quickly discover that I have less and less time and less and less inclination. If I am not breathing in sufficient spiritual oxygen through my lifeline of prayer, I will begin to suffer from spiritual undernourishment. I cannot live a spiritual life without the basic spiritual nourishment that prayer provides. St Alphonsus de Liguori put it this way:

> As moisture is necessary for the life of plants to prevent them from drying up, so, says St Chrysostom, is prayer necessary for our salvation. Prayer vivifies the soul, as the soul vivifies the body. Prayer is called the food of the soul, because the body cannot be supported without food nor can the soul, says St Augustine, be kept alive without prayer. As flesh is nourished by food, so is man supported by prayer. All these comparisons used by the holy Fathers are intended by them to teach the absolute necessity of prayer for the salvation of everyone.[21]

Because prayer is so important for our spiritual well-being, Jesus encourages us to make prayer a priority in our daily schedule with these words:

> So I say to you: Ask, and it will be given to you; search, and you will find; knock, and the door will be opened to you. For the one who asks always receives; the one who searches always finds; the one who knocks will always have the door opened to him. What father among you

would hand his son a stone when he asked for bread? Or hand him a snake instead of a fish? Or hand him a scorpion if he asked for an egg? If you then, who are evil, know how to give your children what is good, how much more will the heavenly Father give the Holy Spirit to those who ask him! (Luke 11:9-13)

The Holy Spirit is the gift that God the Father always wants to give to each of us. We receive this grace and presence of the Spirit when we humbly ask God to pour out his Spirit in our lives.

We would all admit that the special time with God that we call prayer time should normally never take second place to other works. But sometimes that can happen. Prayer can become the last item on the long list of things that have to be done during the day. If this happens, it is both sensible and indeed necessary to examine why it has happened. Then we will be in a position to restore some regularity in our daily pattern of prayer.

A Pattern of Regularity

Some people can organise their prayer life along definite periods of time in the morning and again in the evening or at night. Some people can devote long periods of time to their prayers. Religious brothers and sisters who live in community have definite "community exercises" of prayer each day. I live in such a community and I find those organised times most helpful. They give a good pattern of prayer to our daily life. But the vast majority of people who pray every day do not live in community. You may live alone or with your family. You have to discover the best prayer time for yourself. It doesn't have to be a long period of time. But it is very helpful to have that period in the day when you can say "this is my prayer time". Then you put other things aside, prepare your mind and heart, and spend your designated time with the Lord in prayer.

A pattern of regularity, once established, becomes a great help in living a good prayer life. It ensures that you will be consciously making your way into God's presence every day, usually at the same time, and you will always find the Lord waiting for you. Morning and night prayers are like bookends that hold your day in place. In the morning you welcome the new day as God's gift, and at night you thank him for the way he has been with you and your family during the day and ask his forgiveness for all the times you have not been with him. That rhythm of prayer works well for most people. However, you might be the kind of person for whom it wouldn't work all that well. If so, you have probably found your own best time, or else you are still seeking to discover your best time for your prayer. Whatever the time, it is necessary to ring-fence it and say to yourself, "This is my prayer time and it has priority over all other times."

We are discussing these questions at this stage of the book because the fact that you are reading a book on prayer indicates either that you are a person who prays quite well during the day, or that you want to improve the quality of your prayer time, or that you feel the call to start your life of prayer afresh. You will, I am sure, agree that having definite prayer times during the day would be a great help to the regularity of your prayer life and that it can become a springboard for developing a deeper spiritual life and a deeper commitment to the Lord in your life, as well as a more joyful awareness that you truly are precious in God's sight and that he "has carved you on the palms of his hands" (Isaiah 49:16). But deciding on your own best times can only be done by yourself. However, we know that when we are serious about something in our life we always find good time for it. Time to get up and time to retire, time to eat and time to relax, and, we should surely add, time to pray. Prayer, if we are serious about our relationship with God, should never be in the "when I have time" or "when I feel like it" list of things that we have to do one day.

Our Top Priority

Since prayer is our time with God, our time to be present heart and soul with God, our time for deepening our relationship with God our Father, it should be the top priority on the list of what we have to do each day. And it doesn't have to be a long period of prayer. Busy people begin to discover that even setting aside five minutes in the morning for a quiet time with God sets them up for the day. They have engaged their lifeline. They are off to a good start. They also discover that the five minutes of quiet prayer can be repeated at other times of the day. Their prayer life begins to develop in new ways.

Through the wonderful gift of prayer that God gives, each person has immediate access to all the means for holiness – namely, God's redeeming grace. St Alphonsus' rallying cry was: "He who prays is certainly saved. He who does not pray is certainly lost."[22] For Alphonsus, as indeed for all the great spiritual masters, prayer was as much a necessity for our spiritual life as food is for our bodily life. He would always invite people to look seriously at their prayer life. God has given us the great gift of prayer to secure our sanctification in this world. How are we making use of this gift? Among all the many things I may have to do during the day, is prayer listed as my top priority?

Constant Battle for Prayer

There is an old maxim which says that we pray as well as we live. If we live with some awareness of God, some desire to do what is right and good, to love our neighbour, we are living a good life. When we then turn to God in prayer, our spirit will be at peace in acknowledging that God is our loving Father, that Jesus Christ is our Saviour and Redeemer, our priest who prays in us, and that the Holy Spirit is with us in our weakness. We will be able to relax in God's presence. If we live, however, in forgetfulness of God in our daily life, the chances are that we will simply forget to pray at any time during the day. Prayer is, in the first place, the gift of God, and if we are ignoring God's presence in our life, we will not be aware of the gift he is offering.

We can, too, have very false notions of prayer. Some people think that as they have a busy life to live in the world, they will never have time to pray and they shouldn't be expected to engage in an activity which may be all right for monks or nuns but can have no place in their daily life. People who live by this conviction will often sadly admit that when they retired from their busy life of work they still didn't manage to have time to pray. It is not better time management or some better technique of prayer that we need. Basically, we need a conversion of heart that will enable us to put God first in our life. Jesus put it this way: "Set your hearts on his kingdom first, on God's saving justice, and all these other things will be given you as well" (Matthew 6:33). When we open our hearts to this grace of conversion, which is constantly on offer from God, we begin to discover for ourselves the fulfilment that living a life of prayer brings. Once people begin to realise that something is missing in their life, some deep sense of purpose and meaning, especially as they get on in years, they often open their hearts and receive this great grace from God. Then they begin to feel the need to pray and also the peace that prayer brings to their hearts.

The Catechism of the Catholic Church sums up with the following words many of the challenges we have to overcome in living a life of prayer:

> Our battle has to confront what we experience as *failure in prayer*: discouragement during periods of dryness; sadness that, because we have "great possessions" (Mark 10:22), we have not given all to the Lord; disappointment over not being heard according to our own will; wounded pride, stiffened by the indignity that is ours as sinners; our resistance to the idea that prayer is a free and unmerited gift; and so forth. The conclusion is always the same: what

good does it do to pray? To overcome these obstacles, we must battle to gain humility, trust and perseverance.[23]

The fight is on for a better prayer life in our times, and many people are seeking to secure that for themselves and their families.

Coping with Distractions

People often say to me, "I can't pray. The moment I begin to say my prayers I am assailed with all kinds of thoughts." We call these thoughts distractions. They are part of the prayer experience. Prayer has been traditionally defined as "raising the mind and heart to God". Our heart responds to the gift of prayer and desires to come into God's presence, but the thoughts in our mind can take flight all over the world. We have to remind ourselves regularly that the essence of our prayer does not rest in a perfect *performance*, or in perfect recollection by our mind; rather, it rests in the loving *intention* in our hearts to give the time to God. When we enter into God's presence in our prayer time, God sees the desire in our hearts. He put that desire there. God knows we want to spend this time with him. When we say to ourselves, "It is time for my prayer," God accepts that good intention, and even if our thoughts wander far away from God's presence, our intention to pray remains in place. It is our intention, and not our wandering thoughts, that God sees and accepts. The desire to pray is the very first sign that one is actually living in union with God. That deep desire to pray is God's gift. That desire lifts our hearts up to God. We are already in communion with God.

The fact that our minds wander, that our thoughts are so often about other things, doesn't mean that we have left God's presence. It has been estimated that at least fifty thousand thoughts pass through our minds each day. We have those thoughts, often against our best wishes, and often just fleetingly. We have to say to ourselves, "I am not these thoughts and these thoughts do not take me out of God's presence." We remain where our hearts want to be. Right now our hearts want to be with God in prayer, and those thoughts don't change the desire of our hearts. Each time we become aware that our thoughts are elsewhere we gently let go of the intruding thoughts and refocus on where we are in God's presence. Our thoughts will certainly take flight again. This involuntary distraction, this wandering of our minds, does not undermine our prayer.

Learning from Our Distractions

Some thoughts that we might call distractions may in fact be about the very situations or persons we should be praying for. Not every thought that begins to intrude on my mind during prayer is a distraction. For instance, the thought may be about a situation I would rather not bring to God, or about a person whom I don't really want to think about. Maybe God is saying to me that this situation or this person should be part of my dialogue with God at this time. Then when I bring them before God, asking for God's help, praying for light, those thoughts are no longer distractions but instead have become the substance of my prayer. The distractions may also be telling me something about myself that I would rather not face at this time. They will keep intruding until I take a good look at myself in the presence of God and ask for his help. We can turn distractions to our advantage in our prayer time. But more often than not, the distractions are just of the "wandering thoughts" variety, and we try quietly to let go of them and return to our awareness of the presence of God.

The Catechism of the Catholic Church has this helpful comment to make on distractions:

> The habitual difficulty in prayer is *distraction*. It can affect words and their meaning in vocal prayer; it can concern, more profoundly, him to whom we are praying, in vocal prayer (liturgical or personal), meditation, and contemplative prayer. To set about hunting down

distractions would be to fall into their trap, when all that is necessary is to turn back to our heart: for a distraction reveals to us what we are attached to, and this humble awareness before the Lord should awaken our preferential love for him and lead us resolutely to offer him our heart to be purified. Therein lies the battle, the choice of which master to serve.[24]

A Loving, Contemplative Glance

Each time this happens, as we become aware of these distractions, we gently refocus, bring our minds back to where we are, in the presence of God, and continue peacefully with our prayer. The moment you become aware that your thoughts are elsewhere, that is a moment of grace. The Holy Spirit is reminding you that you can now take a loving, contemplative glance at the Lord Jesus who has come to be with you in this time of prayer. We can turn our very distractions into moments of real contemplation.

It is our thoughts, and not the desire in our heart for our time with God, that are easily distracted. Our heart remains where we want to be. In our time of prayer we want to be with God, at home with Christ. We never allow the distractions to convince us that we cannot pray or that we are wasting our time trying to pray. We remember who is praying for us. Christ is praying in us as our priest, and the Holy Spirit is also interceding for us. So we can confidently enter into our time of prayer and never be discouraged or depressed by our distractions.

Dryness in Our Prayer

Another challenge in living our prayer life is the experience of dryness – lack of appetite for prayer, feelings of tedium and boredom as you try to pray, and time seeming to drag to such an extent that five minutes seem more like thirty. You begin to feel that you are really wasting your time. You could be serving God better if you were out helping people or reading a good book. This is a very subtle and dangerous temptation.

All the great spiritual masters experienced this form of dryness and wrote frequently about how to deal with it. The one thing they all agree on is that we should never cut our prayer time short just because of the tedium and boredom. In fact, St Ignatius Loyola advocates staying a little longer at your prayers when you are battling with this dryness. It is not a question of you having lost God's presence. Rather, God has withdrawn the sense of his presence. We have to learn that this sense of God's absence in our prayer is a deeper spiritual awareness than the sense of God's presence. Only the heart that is yearning for God can experience the pain of his absence. Only the thirsty person longs for a drink of water. Psalm 42 expresses this well: "As the deer longs for running streams, so longs my soul for you, my God" (Psalm 42:1). The sense of God's absence creates a real thirst for God: "My soul thirsts for God, the God of my life; when shall I go to see the face of God?" (Psalm 42:2).

All our struggles with prayer remind us that prayer is a gift of God. Without the grace of the Holy Spirit, which God always gives to those who ask him, we cannot pray. Jesus made this very clear when he said, "I am the vine, you are the branches. Whoever remains in me with me in him bears fruit in plenty; for cut off from me you can do nothing" (John 15:5).

If we prepare our hearts and minds for our prayer time; if we seek to the best of our ability to develop a regular pattern of daily prayer, no matter how short; if we refuse to allow the experience of distractions or dryness to convince us that that we cannot pray, we will be living a life of prayer, and our lifeline to God will be engaged each day. We will be able to say with St Alphonsus, "And for myself, I speak the truth, I never feel greater consolation, nor greater confidence of my salvation, than when I am praying to God, and recommending myself to him."[25]

❖

— Chapter 3 —

Jesus Teaches Us How to Pray

When the disciples asked Jesus to teach them how to pray, he taught them – and he teaches us – the prayer we call "the Lord's Prayer", the Our Father. Jesus' words and his teaching don't belong to the past like the words of Plato or Shakespeare. Jesus' words are the words of God, spoken to us today, just as they were spoken two thousand years ago, to his first disciples. As the author of the Letter to the Hebrews said, "The word of God is something alive and active" (Hebrews 4:12). God's word, Jesus' word, is a living and a life-giving word. When Jesus speaks the word of God in the Gospel he is speaking directly to us in the present. He is saying to us today, "You should pray like this: Our Father…" (Matthew 6:9). The first word we speak to God when we come into his presence is Father: *Our Father*. That is how Jesus teaches us to relate in prayer to our God.

Prayer is first and foremost our response to God's invitation and grace. We try and give our full attention to the Lord, who is present with us, teaching us how to pray, giving us the words of the Our Father to speak to God in our prayer. Each word of the Our Father is rich in meaning and gives us a glimpse into the mystery of God and into the relationship that God wishes to have with us. God invites us to come to him in prayer because he is our loving Father and he wants us to open our hearts to him, asking for everything we need for our life. Jesus tells us to come to God in prayer with the sentiment of a child in our hearts and the word of a child on our lips, and say *Abba, Father*.

We don't just say the words of the Our Father. We assimilate the meaning of the words and then the words gradually form within us the very attitudes of Jesus. St Paul says to us, "Make your own the mind of Christ" (Philippians 2:5). And he also says to us, quoting scripture, "*Who has ever known the mind of the Lord? Who has ever been his adviser?* But we are those who have the mind of Christ" (1 Corinthians 2:16). The mind of Christ, the very attitude of Christ towards God and towards our neighbours, is formed in us as we pray the Lord's Prayer.

The Structure of the Lord's Prayer

St Matthew and St Luke both give us accounts of how Jesus taught his disciples to pray. There are slight variations between these two Gospel accounts. The Church chose St Matthew's version of the Lord's Prayer for her daily prayer in the Mass. It is Matthew's version that we all learn and say when we pray the Lord's Prayer.[26] Before we look at the individual words we speak to God in the Lord's Prayer, let us take a brief look at the structure of the prayer in St Matthew's Gospel. It consists of seven petitions. The first three petitions are about God: *his name*, *his kingdom* and *his will*. The last four petitions are about us: *give us*, *forgive us*, *lead us* and *deliver us*. All these petitions are addressed to God as Our Father. It is worth noting that Jesus gives us this beautiful prayer while preaching his famous Sermon on the Mount which we find in chapters 5, 6 and 7 of Matthew's Gospel. In this sermon, Jesus refers to God as Father seventeen times. In the middle of this great sermon, in chapter 6, he teaches us to pray to God as our Father and gives us the Lord's Prayer.

We Dare to Call Him Father

While celebrating Mass, the priest introduces this wonderful prayer with these words: "At the Saviour's command and formed by divine teaching we dare to say: Our Father, who art in heaven." We dare to call God our Father because Jesus our redeemer tells us that we can and should speak to God his Father and our Father in this familial way. It is Jesus who reveals to us that God is our loving Father. He said to his disciples, "No one knows the Son except the Father, just as no one knows the Father except the Son and those to whom the

Son chooses to reveal him" (Matthew 11:27).

Jesus has chosen to reveal God the Father to us, and he teaches us to call God *our Father*. The fact that we dare to call God our Father is due entirely to the revelation that we have received in our hearts. It is the gift of faith, the inner light of faith that enables us to see beyond all the circumstances of our life to the very source of our existence, to God our Creator and our Father. All our existence, all our being comes ultimately from God. As we pray in the psalms: "You created my inmost self, knit me together in my mother's womb. For so many marvels I thank you; a wonder am I, and all your works are wonders" (Psalm 139:13-14).

By revealing to us that God is our loving Father, Jesus seeks to engage our hearts. He reveals the intimate and personal relationship each one of us has with God. It is that personal relationship that the human heart yearns for. The question then is not "how do I think about God?", but "how do I relate to God?" It is in and through that relationship that we have access to God in our prayer. The way of the heart is different from the way of the head. In our prayer, in our search for the presence of God in our life, we follow the way of the heart. As the seventeenth-century French philosopher Blaise Pascal said, "the heart has its reasons which reason knows nothing about".[27]

What is that deep restlessness in the human heart? Where does it come from? After years of searching to discover the meaning of his restlessness, St Augustine burst forth with this classic explanation:

> Too late have I loved you, O Beauty so ancient and so new, too late have I loved you. Behold, you were within me, while I was outside; it was there that I sought you, and, a deformed creature, rushed headlong upon these things of beauty which you have made. You were with me, but I was not with you. They kept me apart from you, those fair things which, if they were not in you, would not exist at all. You have called to me, and cried out, and have shattered

51

my deafness. You blazed forth with light, and have shone upon me, and you have put blindness to flight. You have sent forth fragrance, and I have drawn my breath, and I pant after you. I have tasted you, and I hunger and thirst after you. You have touched me, and I have burned for your peace.[28]

Jesus speaks directly to that restlessness in Augustine's heart and every human heart when he tells us to come to God with the sentiment of a child in our hearts and the word of a child on our lips and say *Abba, Father*. As St Paul said, "As you are sons, God has sent into our hearts the Spirit of his Son crying, *Abba*, Father" (Galatians 4:6). That beautiful and intimate word "Father" is already spoken in our hearts by the Holy Spirit even before we come to pray to God. It is very helpful to be still and to listen to the Spirit of God saying, "Abba, Father" in our hearts. Then you can join your voice with the voice of the Spirit and begin your Our Father.

Prayer is coming into God's presence, but sometimes we forget that God is present in our hearts, where the Spirit is crying out, *Abba, Father*, and we try to seek God somewhere else. Then we fail to find him. We have the experience that St Augustine discovered: "You were within me while I was outside." To avoid seeking God in the wrong place, the first thing we should try to do, as we begin our prayer, is to enter into our hearts and be still, even for a few moments. Now we are ready to speak to our Father, who is in our hearts.

Our Father

We don't come to God in our prayer as isolated individuals, each of us concerned only for ourselves. We come to God as God's family. That is why we say *our* Father, not *my* Father. God recognises every human being as his child. When we use the words *our Father* we are taking our place in the family of God. We are including in that word *our* every human being. By beginning our prayer with the words *Our Father* we recognise our solidarity with all the children of God our

Father, even with those who may not like us or who may even be enemies. By revealing God to us as our Father, Jesus simultaneously reveals our true dignity as God's sons and daughters. The Second Vatican Council said: "Christ the new Adam, in the very revelation of the mystery of the Father and of his love, fully reveals men and women to themselves and brings to light their very high calling."[29]

We make this teaching our own by simply saying, "Jesus Christ fully reveals me to myself." Only Christ can tell us who we truly are. By revealing to us that God is our Father, Jesus reveals to us that we are sons and daughters of God. As Pope Francis put it: Our surname is God.[30]

In our time of prayer we begin by expressing our faith in who God is: he is our loving Father. We also express our faith in who we are: we are God's sons and daughters. There is no human being born into this world who does not have Jesus Christ as a brother. We can, therefore, unite ourselves with the whole human race as we begin to pray, *Our Father*. In a special way we unite ourselves with all our Christian brothers and sisters as we say this great prayer that Jesus teaches us. But now we have to attune our hearts and minds to our voices. We have to mean what we say when we begin to talk to God in prayer. We cannot claim that God is our Father while excluding other groups, other races or even one individual.

We should also be aware that in calling God our Father we are also including all the tenderness of God as Mother. Again, the Catechism makes this helpful comment:

> By calling God "Father", the language of faith indicates two things: that God is first origin of everything and transcendent authority; and that he is at the same time goodness and loving care for all his children. God's parental tenderness can also be expressed by the image of motherhood, which emphasises God's immanence, the intimacy between Creator and creature.[31]

If the image of father doesn't speak to someone about the goodness and love of God, the image of mother may do so. In the scriptures, God compares himself to a mother in this way: "You will be suckled, carried on her hip and fondled in her lap. As a mother comforts a child, so I shall comfort you" (Isaiah 66:12-13). And in the psalms we read: "Like a little child in its mother's arms, like a little child, so I keep myself" (Psalm 131:2). Jesus, in revealing God to us as our Father, calls us into an intimate, trusting, loving relationship with our heavenly Father. Sadly, as Pope Benedict XVI pointed out, the image of father is not always a comforting one:

> It is true, of course, that contemporary men and women have difficulty in experiencing the great consolation of the word father immediately, since the experience of father is in many cases either completely absent or obscured by inadequate examples of fatherhood.[32]

There can be a wound in the heart, a "father wound", a space left empty because of the absence of one's father, the absence of a father's love, encouragement and compassion. But that wound in the heart of God's son or daughter will be healed if they bring it into God's presence and say, "Father, gracious Father, loving Father," and allow the Father's love to embrace them. While our earthly fathers may not have been perfect, our heavenly Father is full of love, mercy and compassion for each of us. The Lord assures us that "he has come to bind up the broken heart" (Isaiah 61:1).

Who Art in Heaven

When we say "God is in heaven", we are not talking about some place far from our earth. Heaven is where God is and God dwells with us and in us. Jesus says to us, "Anyone who loves me will keep my word and my Father will love him and we will come to him and make our home in him" (John 14:23).

In our prayer we are not trying to escape from the earth to reach God in some place that we call heaven. Rather, we are entering into our hearts, where God dwells. As Jesus says to us, "But when you pray, *go into your private room, shut yourself in, and pray* to your Father who is in that secret place, and your Father who sees all that is done in secret will reward you" (Matthew 6:6). We can say, then, that when we pray we are consciously dwelling with God in our hearts. As St John says, "God is love and whoever remains in love remains in God and God in him" (1 John 4:16). Heaven is where God is; God dwells in our hearts; when we pray "Our Father, who art in heaven" we enter our hearts to be at home with God. St Augustine expressed this well when he wrote: "Our Father who art in heaven is rightly understood to mean that God is in the hearts of the just, as in his holy temple."[33]

Hallowed Be Thy Name

Having acknowledged who God truly is, our Father who dwells with us and in us, we now pray that God will do three things for the glory of his name. We ask him to *hallow his name*; we pray that *his kingdom comes*; we also pray that *his will be done*. We look at each of these separately.

When we say, "hallowed be thy name", what are we asking God to do? This is how the great Father of the Church, Tertullian, explained it, writing in the third century:

> When we say "hallowed be thy name", we ask that it should be hallowed in us, who are in him; but also in others whom God's grace still awaits, that we may obey the precept that obliges us to pray for everyone, even our enemies. That is why we do not say expressly "hallowed be thy name 'in us'", for we ask that it be so in all people.[34]

We are in the presence of God our Father as we say "hallowed be thy name". God promised to hallow his name in us when he said:

I am going to display the holiness of my great name which has been profaned among the nations, which you have profaned among them... I shall pour clean water over you and you will be cleansed; I shall cleanse you of all your filth and all your foul idols. I shall give you a new heart, and put a new spirit in you; I shall remove your heart of stone and give you a heart of flesh instead. I shall put my spirit in you, and make you keep my laws and respect and practise my judgements. You will live in the country I gave your ancestors. You shall be my people and I shall be your God. (Ezekiel 36:23-28)

That is how God hallows his name; he gives us his Spirit and cleanses us from all our sins. When we pray *hallowed be thy name* we are asking God to fulfil all his great promises. God knows our hearts and everything that is going on in our lives, good or bad. When we say *hallowed be thy name* we are inviting God "to pour clean water over us and cleanse of all our sins"; we are asking "for the new heart and the new spirit". Right at the beginning of this great prayer we are opening our whole lives to God. From time to time we can very profitably stop at this point and just repeat, slowly in our heart, over and over again: *Our Father who art in heaven, hallowed be thy name.*

Thy Kingdom Come

We now pray for God's kingdom to come. How do we visualise this kingdom? What is it? St Pope John Paul II gives us his answer in his encyclical letter on the Mission of the Church:

The kingdom of God is not a concept, a doctrine, or a programme subject to free interpretation, but it is before all else *a person* with the face and name of Jesus of Nazareth, the image of the invisible God. If the kingdom is separated from Jesus, it is no longer the kingdom of God which he revealed.[35]

The kingdom comes in human hearts, not in political territories. In this great request we are asking God the Father for the saving presence of Jesus, our Redeemer, to be with us in every situation of our lives. The kingdom of God is present in hearts that are touched and transformed by Christ's saving grace. As St Paul says, "The kingdom of God does not mean eating or drinking this or that, it means righteousness and peace and joy brought by the Holy Spirit" (Romans 14:17). When we pray, then, for the kingdom of God to come, we are asking for the Holy Spirit to come into our lives and fill us with peace and joy.

Jesus tells us that seeking God's kingdom is the priority of our lives: "Set your hearts on God's kingdom first, and on God's saving justice, and all these other things will be given you as well. So do not worry about tomorrow: tomorrow will take care of itself" (Matthew 6:33-34). While praying *Thy kingdom come*, we are invited to hand over all our worries and troubles of any kind to God so that God's peace can enter our hearts. We can profitably spend some time with God simply saying *Thy kingdom come*. We don't have to say all the words of the Lord's Prayer at once. When you are praying this great prayer on your own you can profitably stop at each of the seven petitions and take some time to meditate more deeply on each one. Each of the petitions gives us food for thought, meditation and contemplation.

Thy Will be Done on Earth as it is in Heaven

If we pray to do God's will, how can we know his will? This is a very big question for everyone who believes in God. The Second Vatican Council answered it in this way:

> Deep within his conscience man discovers a law which he has not laid upon himself but which he must obey. Its voice, ever calling him to love and do what is good and avoid evil, tells him inwardly at the right moment: do this,

shun that. For man has in his heart a law inscribed by God. His dignity lies in observing this law, and by it he will be judged. His conscience is man's most secret core, and his sanctuary. There he is alone with God whose voice echoes in his depths.[36]

Through the gift of our conscience God guides us on our pilgrim journey in this world. God speaks to us through our conscience. We learn at an early age to "follow our conscience" or "never go against our conscience". Indeed, we learned that acting against our conscience is what we call sin. The Catechism gives us this helpful definition of sin:

> Sin is an offence against reason, truth and right conscience; it is failure in genuine love of God and neighbour caused by a perverse attachment to certain goods. It wounds the nature of man and injures human solidarity.[37]

Acting against our conscience is denying our true dignity. It always inflicts a wound on our inner being, undermines our true self-esteem and robs our heart of true peace and joy. That is why Jesus teaches us to pray "Thy will be done", because only in God's will can we find true human fulfilment and peace of heart.

God's will is "for everyone to be saved and reach full knowledge of the truth" (1 Timothy 2:4). God wants each person to know his will because it is the supreme good in our lives. Nothing is good which is contrary to God's will. When we pray, "Thy will be done," we are not saying my will be done, or our will be done. God our Father's will for each of us is perfect. God never wills what is not good for us, even though we may be tempted at times to say, "What have I done to deserve this?" when things go wrong in our lives. When we pray, we are asking God to conform our wills to his holy will. We can receive no greater blessing from God than this conformity of our will with his divine will. God our loving Father wills only what is truly best for each of us. And so we can pray with great confidence, "Thy will be done."

Jesus is the man in whom God's will was perfectly fulfilled. He said of himself, "Here I am... I am coming to do your will, God" (Hebrews 10:7). He also said to his disciples, "My food is to do the will of the one who sent me, and to complete his work" (John 4:34). And in the midst of his agony in the garden he cried out to God, "Let your will not mine be done" (Luke 22:42).

Jesus did God's will on earth just as it is done in heaven. Heaven is the place where God's will is done. When God's will is done on earth, earth becomes heaven. As Pope Benedict XVI said:

> Earth becomes "heaven" when and insofar as God's will is done there; and it is merely "earth", the opposite of heaven, when and insofar as it withdraws from the will of God. This is why we pray that it may be done on earth as it is in heaven – that earth may become "heaven".[38]

Just visualise for a moment what our world would be like to live in if everyone did the will of God and lived a life of sincere love, even for their enemies. St Paul tells us, "Love can cause no harm to your neighbour, and so love is the fulfilment of the law" (Romans 13:10). Where everyone loved one another we would have heaven on earth.

Give Us This Day Our Daily Bread

As we have seen, the first three petitions of the Lord's Prayer are about God – about his name, his kingdom and his will. These petitions precede our petitions for ourselves. This is the right order of prayer. As the Catechism points out:

> The Lord's Prayer is the most perfect of prayers. In it we ask, not only for all the things we rightly desire, but also in the sequence that they should be desired. This prayer teaches us not only to ask for things, but also in what order we should desire them.[39]

Having put God's name, God's kingdom and God's will first in our petitions, we now make the fourth petition, the first "give us" petition. We pray for "our daily bread". The meaning of this phrase is not immediately obvious from our English translation. When we hear the words "daily bread" we probably think immediately of the bread we need for our breakfast, the bread you may bake yourself or buy in some supermarket. But the New Testament Greek word, translated as 'daily' in our modern Bibles, is *epiousios*, a word which occurs only once in the New Testament, in the Lord's Prayer, and which occurs nowhere else in Greek literature. This kind of word is called a *hapax legomenon*, defined by the Oxford English Dictionary as "a word of which only one instance of its use is recorded". It is a word which the Lord Jesus chose specifically to describe the bread we pray for in the Lord's Prayer. In the fifth century, St Jerome, the great Greek scholar, translated the word *epiousios* as *super-substantial* in his translation of the Hebrew and Greek Scriptures into Latin. His translation became known as the Latin Vulgate Bible, and for centuries it was the official version of the Bible in the Church. During the turbulent years of the Protestant Reformation when English priests had to go to the Continent to study for the priesthood, an English translation of the Latin Vulgate Bible was begun in the English College in Douai, in Belgium. The New Testament was published in English in 1582. It faithfully followed St Jerome's translation of *epiousios* as super-substantial. In its translation of the Our Father we read "give us this day our super-substantial bread". Modern translations of the Bible prefer to translate *epiousios* as "our daily bread". But Pope Benedict XVI commented: "The Fathers of the Church were practically unanimous in understanding the fourth petition of the Our Father (for our daily bread) as a Eucharistic petition; in this sense the Our Father figures in the Mass liturgy as a Eucharistic table-prayer (i.e. 'grace')."[40]

If we think that we are only asking for a loaf of bread we have lost the deeper meaning of the word *epiousios*. In this fourth petition of the Our Father we are asking for everything that sustains our life, both bodily and spiritually – for that super-substantial food that we need to live the full life that Jesus wants us to live in this world. He said, "I have come that they may have life and have it to the full" (John 10:10). Without that "bread of life" that we pray for, that *epiousios* bread, the bread of the Eucharist, our lives will be less than full. That is why we make this request to God in the Lord's Prayer.

The Catechism of the Catholic Church helps us to reclaim the original meaning of the word now translated as "daily":

> "Daily" (*epiousios*) occurs nowhere else in the New Testament. Taken in a temporal sense, this word is a pedagogical repetition of "this day", to confirm us in trust "without reservation". Taken in the qualitative sense, it signifies what is necessary for life, and more broadly every good thing sufficient for subsistence. Taken literally (*epiousios*: "super-essential"), it refers directly to the Bread of Life, the Body of Christ, the "medicine of immortality", without which we have no life within us. Finally in this connection, its heavenly meaning is evident: "this day" is the Day of the Lord, the day of the feast of the kingdom, anticipated in the Eucharist that is already the foretaste of the kingdom to come. For this reason it is fitting for the Eucharistic liturgy to be celebrated each day.[41]

It is good to spend some time on this first "give us" petition. We are asking for the bread of life, the bread that Jesus came to give us. He says of himself, "I am the living bread which has come down from heaven. Anyone who eats this bread will live for ever; and the bread that I will give is my flesh for the life of the world" (John 6:51).

Forgive Us Our Trespasses as We Forgive Those Who Trespass Against Us

As we stand before God, acknowledging him as "our Father" and acknowledging ourselves "as his sons and daughters", we ask for our "Eucharistic bread" and the forgiveness of our sins. But then we make our forgiveness of others the measure of the forgiveness that we will receive from God. We say "forgive us as we forgive". That can be a very challenging prayer to say, especially if we are going through a difficult time with someone. We must include everyone in that *our* of the Our Father. Even our greatest enemy and all the people who may not like us or those whom we may not like – all are included as we stand and address God as "our Father". This petition in the Our Father is so important that Jesus re-emphasises it when he says, "Yes, if you forgive others their failings, your heavenly Father will forgive you yours; but if you do not forgive others, your Father will not forgive your failings either" (Matthew 6:14-15).

It requires great honesty on our part to make this fifth petition of the Lord's Prayer and mean it. Are we willing to ask God to make our forgiveness of others the measure of the forgiveness he gives to us? That is what we say when we say "as we forgive". We need to allow these words, this condition of our own forgiveness by God, to sink into our hearts. It is a serious request with very serious implications. I need to honestly ask myself this question: do I prefer holding on to unforgiveness of the person who has wronged me to receiving God's forgiveness of all my own sins? It is a very big choice.

We have to remind ourselves of the important distinction between the broken heart that feels it cannot forgive and the hardened heart that is determined not to forgive. The broken heart needs healing; the hardened heart needs conversion.

It is only forgiveness that heals the broken heart. There is no other medicine. If we are sincerely praying "forgive us as we forgive them" and we realise that there is someone we have not forgiven and we ask for the grace to forgive, we will always receive it from God. But if we are saying "forgive us as we forgive them" and we realise that we are determined never to forgive, we have to sincerely pray for the grace of conversion, for the gift of the new heart. We humbly ask God to fulfil his great promise: "I will take from your body the heart of stone and give you a new heart" (Ezekiel 36:26). Only God can give us a new heart, and as we persist in this request God always grants it.

Lead Us Not into Temptation

We believe that Christ died to save us from our sins. We can therefore find it very puzzling that this sixth petition of the Our Father says to God: *lead us not into temptation*. Surely God would never do that? Modern translations of the Greek New Testament render this petition in this way: do not put us to the test. As the Catechism of the Catholic Church points out: "It is difficult to translate the Greek verb used by a single English word: the Greek means both 'do not allow us to enter into temptation' and 'do not let us yield to temptation'."[42] Commenting on the words *lead us not*, the *New Jerome Biblical Commentary* states: "This probably means 'do not let us succumb to the end-time trial' or 'do not let us fall when we are tempted'."[43]

We make this request to not be put to the test or led into temptation after we have prayed for the forgiveness of our own sins. St James says:

> Never, when you are being put to the test, say, "God is tempting me"; God cannot be tempted by evil, and he does not put anyone to the test. Everyone is put to the test by being attracted and seduced by that person's wrong desire. Then the desire conceives and gives birth to sin, and when sin reaches its full growth, it gives birth to death. (James 1:13-15)

Temptation is a very common human experience. Even Jesus was tempted by the devil during his forty days in the desert. But he never yielded to those temptations. Jesus understands, therefore, what it means to be tempted. As scripture says, "For the high priest we have is not incapable of feeling our weaknesses with us, but has been put to the test in exactly the same way as ourselves, apart from sin" (Hebrews 4:15). That is why Jesus teaches us in the Lord's Prayer to ask the Father not to put us to the test. Jesus knows our weakness and he knows that in times of temptation, if we don't turn to God for help, we can easily yield to the temptation. If we run to God for help in the midst of temptation, then we can put all our trust in God's help. As St Paul says, "You can trust that God will not let you be put to the test beyond your strength, but with any trial will provide a way out by enabling you to put up with it" (1 Corinthians 10:13). The experience of being tempted can become for us a clarion call to pray. If we respond to that call and seek God's help, we will not be overcome by temptation.

Deliver Us from Evil

In this final petition in the Lord's Prayer, Jesus teaches us to ask the Father to deliver us from evil. We pray, "Lead us not into temptation but deliver us from evil." Rather than putting us to the test, we implore the Father to deliver us from the Evil One. Jesus not only taught us to pray for this deliverance, he himself also prayed that we would be delivered from evil. During his great high-priestly prayer at the Last Supper he prayed: "I am not asking you to remove them from this world, but to protect them from the Evil One" (John 17:15). Jesus was fully aware that the devil exists. He warned us that the devil seeks to deceive us by speaking lies and distorting the truth: "He was a murderer from the start; he was never grounded in the truth; there is no truth at all in him. When he lies he is speaking true to his nature because he is a liar and the father of lies" (John 8:44).

St John tells us, "This was the purpose of the appearing of the Son of God, to undo the work of the devil" (1 John 3:8). Through his great love for us, by his death and resurrection, Jesus has undone the work of the devil and now he continues to pray to the Father that we will be protected from that evil one. But he invites us to join in that prayer. That is why he teaches us to pray, "Deliver us from evil." St Peter says to us, "Be sober and alert, because your enemy the devil is on the prowl like a roaring lion, looking for someone to devour. Stand up to him, strong in faith" (1 Peter 5:8-9). St James assures us with these words: "Give in to God, then; resist the devil and he will run away from you" (James 4:7). The devil is a coward, a defeated, fallen spirit, and he is much more afraid of us than we should be of him. When he sees us he always sees the "image of God", the very body of Christ in this world.

We pray for God to deliver us from evil with great confidence because, as St Paul reassures us:

> I am certain of this: neither death nor life, nor angels, nor principalities, nothing already in existence and nothing still to come nor any power, nor heights nor the depths, nor any created thing whatever, will be able to come between us and the love of God, known to us in Christ Jesus our Lord. (Romans 8:38-39)

The Church, in the Mass, prays each day for deliverance from evil. After the community has prayed the Lord's Prayer, the priest continues: "Deliver us, Lord, we pray, from every evil, graciously grant peace in our days, that by the help of your mercy we may be always free from sin and safe from all distress, as we await the blessed hope and the coming of our Saviour Jesus Christ." The Church takes very seriously the reality of evil in our world. That is why Jesus taught us to pray for deliverance from evil and why the Church continues, in her official prayers, to pray for that deliverance.

Now that we have come to the end of our reflection on each of the seven petitions of the Lord's Prayer, you might find it helpful to say the whole prayer again to God our Father, lingering for a few moments on the petitions that may speak to you in a new way.

— Chapter 4 —

The Hail Mary

After the Lord's Prayer, the Hail Mary is the best-known and best-loved prayer for Catholics worldwide. Thanks to the ecumenical spirit that has filled many of the Christian churches in the past fifty years, a growing number of members of the other churches have begun to foster devotion to Our Lady, and some of them are happy to ask Mary's intercession by using the words of the Hail Mary. As a prayer, not only is it full of warm, filial devotion to our Mother Mary, but it is also a profession of our faith in the Father, the Son and the Holy Spirit. It is, as we will see, a Trinitarian and a Christocentric prayer. It is a prayer that engages both heart and head – it is a recognition of our loving relationship with the Mother of Our Lord Jesus Christ and a profession of our faith in his divinity and his conception in his Mother's womb through the power of the Holy Spirit.

Attuning Our Minds to Our Voices

Since the Hail Mary may be the prayer we say most frequently during the day, it is important that we try to give our full attention to both the words and the sentiments expressed in this beautiful prayer. While we can give our assent to each word we are saying without thinking specifically about the meaning of each word, it is also very helpful, from time to time, to take the prayer slowly and reflect on each word. We try, in the words of the Second Vatican Council, "to attune our minds to our voices",[44] to mean what we are saying and to give our full consent to what we are saying. When we come to pray it is always necessary for us to become more consciously aware of what we are doing. Again, it is worth repeating that the essence of our prayer is in the desire to give the time, even though, as we saw in an earlier chapter, we experience distractions of all kinds and may well have finished the prayer before we even thought about a single word of it. In our prayer time we are consciously seeking to engage our lifeline and breathe in the spiritual oxygen of the prayer. As we cross the threshold of prayer we are entering into the presence of God our Father; we are opening our whole life in faith to receive the gift of the Father's blessing; we are asking Christ our Lord to give us the gift of the Holy Spirit; we are going to live by "every word that comes from the mouth of God" (Matthew 4:4). When we are praying the Hail Mary we are seeking to live by those last words which Jesus spoke to us on earth, just before he died on the cross for us – namely, "She is your mother" (John 19:27). Pope Francis comments:

> These words of the dying Jesus are not chiefly the expression of his devotion and concern for his mother; rather, they are a revelatory formula which manifests the mystery of a special, saving mission. Jesus left us his mother to be our mother. Only after doing so did Jesus know that "all was now finished" (John 19:28). At the foot of the cross, at the supreme hour of the new creation, Christ led us to Mary.[45]

It is good to remind ourselves that when we honour the mother of Jesus as our mother, we are expressing our faith in those final words that Jesus spoke from the cross. If Jesus had not said to the beloved disciple at the foot of the cross, "She is your mother," the Church would never have been led by the Holy Spirit to develop and promote its strong and fervent devotion to Mary. The Orthodox Church shares with the Catholic Church this strong devotion to Mary. The Orthodox bishop Kallistos Ware said:

> That we should turn to Mary in prayer seems to an Orthodox Christian something altogether natural and inevitable. For him there is nothing exotic or polemical about such prayer. But it forms an integral and unquestioned part of his life in

Christ... For Orthodoxy, this prayer springs quite simply from the sense of "belonging together", from the feeling that she and we are members of the same fellowship, that she is Mother within the great Christian family of which we are also part. She and we belong to the one Church, and the unity of that Church is a unity of prayer – that, in a word, is why we ask her to pray for us.[46]

Before Jesus was conceived in his mother's womb, God the Father greeted Mary through the archangel Gabriel with the words, "Hail, full of grace, the Lord is with you" (Luke 1:28). God acknowledged that she was the one person in the world who was full of grace. As Jesus was about to leave this world he spoke to his mother at the foot of the cross and said to her, "He is your son," and to the disciple he said, "She is your mother" (John 19:26-27). The woman whom God the Father called "full of grace" now has, through the words of her Son, a new grace and a new office: she has become the mother of all disciples. That is why devotion to Mary developed at such an early stage in the Church. She herself had foretold it: "All generations will call me blessed" (Luke 1:48). When we turn to Mary and greet her with the words "Hail full of grace" we are joining our voices with the voice of God the Father and we are opening our hearts to the great mystery of the Incarnation of God the Son in her womb through the power of the Holy Spirit. She is the mother of Jesus; she is the mother of each disciple; she is the mother of the Church.

Speaking of her motherhood, the Second Vatican Council said:

This motherhood of Mary in the order of grace continues without interruption from the consent which she loyally gave at the Annunciation and which she sustained without wavering beneath the cross, until the eternal fulfilment of all the elect. Taken up into heaven she did not lay aside this saving office but by her manifold intercession continues to bring us the gifts of eternal salvation. By her motherly

69

love she cares for her Son's sisters and brothers who still journey on earth surrounded by dangers and difficulties, until they are led into their blessed home. Therefore the Blessed Virgin is invoked in the Church under the titles of Advocate, Helper, Benefactress, and Mediatrix. This, however, is understood in such a way that it neither takes away anything from, nor adds anything to, the dignity and efficacy of Christ the one Mediator.[47]

The Council's teaching gives us the reason why we cultivate devotion to our Blessed Mother. She is interceding for us with her Son. We can commit all our needs, all our hopes and fears, our families, everyone we love to her motherly intercession. Let us reflect on the words we speak when we say this great prayer.

Hail Mary

The word "hail" is first of all a greeting. We are greeting Mary by her name. Our very greeting means that we are aware that we have come into the presence of Mary. We never say "Hail" or "Greetings" to someone who is not present. The fact that we begin our prayer with "Hail Mary" means that we believe that we are now in the presence of Mary our mother. She is present to us in the whole mystery of God. Because Mary, in body and soul, in her whole person, is now with Christ in heaven, she can relate to each of her spiritual children on earth in an individual and personal way. Heaven, as we saw in the last chapter, is where God is, and God is with us. In the new creation, where God is all in all, Mary can now have a personal relationship with all the members of Christ's body on earth, with the Church. She knows each of us by name. We are not strangers to our mother in heaven. Because of her glorious assumption, her complete transformation in Christ, Mary is now present as mother to each of us in the mystery of Christ, in the mystery of the Church. So when we say "Hail Mary" she hears us, she listens to us and she is ever ready to help us. As St Pope John Paul II wrote:

Mary is present in the Church as the Mother of Christ, and at the same time as that mother whom Christ, in the mystery of the Redemption, gave to humanity in the person of the Apostle John. Thus, in her new motherhood in the Spirit, Mary embraces each and every one *in* the Church, and embraces each and every one *through* the Church.[48]

Kecharitomene: full of grace

The beautiful description of Mary, "full of grace", was first given by God the Father when he sent the archangel Gabriel to invite her to become the mother of Our Lord Jesus Christ. The archangel didn't call her Mary, the name by which we know her. He gave her a new name. He called her, in Greek, the original language of the Gospel, *kecharitomene*, a word that we have traditionally translated as "full of grace". The great scripture scholar Ignace de La Potterie comments: "The Fathers of the Church such as Origen and Ambrose make the observation that in the entire Bible the form *kecharitomene* is only applied to Mary."[49]

The angel said, "Rejoice, so highly favoured," or, in our traditional translation, "Hail, full of grace" (Luke 1:28). Mary is the one who has been transformed by grace. Before God asked her to become the mother of Jesus, Mary had been transformed by grace. She could truly say with St Paul, "Blessed be the God and Father of our Lord Jesus Christ, who has blessed us with all the spiritual blessings of heaven in Christ. Even before the world was made God chose us…" (Ephesians 1:3-4). The living tradition of the Church tells us that this transforming power of grace was at work in Mary right from the first moment of her existence. Mary was never in "the state of sin", never alienated from God through original sin or actual sin. God's grace, which transforms and makes holy, was always effective in Mary. Mary stands out as the one who depends totally on God's grace and not on her own merits. In the presence of God, from the very first moment of her conception, that is who Mary is: she is the graced one, the transformed and holy one. She is *kecharitomene*. St Pope John Paul II said: "He calls her thus as if it were her real name. He does not call her by her proper earthly name: Miryam (Mary) but *by this new name: 'full of grace'*."[50]

The Lord Is with You

In presenting Mary as the one who has been transformed by grace, Luke is showing us how God prepared her for her vocation, her mission and her role in the work of our salvation. Mary was troubled by this new name, *kecharitomene*, full of grace. St Luke writes: "She was deeply disturbed by these words and asked herself what this greeting could mean" (Luke 1:29). Knowing that she was disturbed by his greeting, the archangel spoke to her again and this time he called her by her own name, the name her parents had given her. He said, "Mary, do not be afraid, you have found God's favour" (Luke 1:30). Gabriel is telling Mary that she has a special relationship with the God of her fathers, of Abraham, Isaac and Jacob. God is with her and she is with God. And God has a special mission for her: "You are to conceive in your womb and bear a son, and you must call him Jesus. He will be great and will be called the Son of the Most High. The Lord God will give him the throne of his ancestor David: he will rule over the House of Jacob for ever and his reign will have no end" (Luke 1:31-33). Mary doesn't doubt this extraordinary word of the angel but she asks for clarification: "How can this come about since I am a virgin?" (Luke 1:34). It is a very reasonable question to ask, and she got her answer: "The Holy Spirit will come upon you and the power of the Most High will cover you with its shadow. And so the child will be holy and will be called Son of God" (Luke 1:35). And Mary, the woman whom God calls full of grace, *kecharitomene*, accepts her new vocation to become the mother of the Son of God, accepts the mission that God has for her, accepts whatever role God wishes her to play. She says, "I am the servant of the Lord, let it happen to me as you have said" (Luke 1:38).

Our traditional translation of Mary's response, which we still use in the Angelus, is "Be it done unto me according to thy word." This well-known response of Mary can be interpreted as meaning that she was merely passive and resigned. On the contrary, far from being passively resigned, she was actively engaged in entering into a partnership with God. As John McHugh points out, the correct translation of "let it be done unto me" is a cry of joy, "O may it be so for me, according to thy word." McHugh notes that the verb "let it be done" is in the optative mood in Greek, which is used to express a wish or a desire.[51] And Ignace de La Potterie comments:

> The "fiat" (let it be done unto me) of Mary is not just a simple acceptance and even less, a resignation. It is rather a joyous desire to collaborate with what God foresees for her. It is the joy of total abandonment to the good will of God. Thus the joy of this ending responds to the invitation to joy at the beginning.[52]

Having heard God's explanation of how she was to become the mother of Jesus, Mary yearned to see God's plan fulfilled. Oh yes, let the Holy Spirit come, is her answer to the angel. She was not just a passive recipient of the divine plan. She was an active, intelligent and courageous collaborator with God. In the words of St Paul, we were at the "appointed time", God's time, the "fullness of time" when Mary said her definitive yes to God. Paul wrote, "When the appointed time came, God sent his Son, born of a woman, born under the Law, to redeem the subjects of the Law and to enable us to be adopted as Sons" (Galatians 4:4-5).[53]

Blessed Art Thou Among Women

Our prayer now moves from Nazareth – where the archangel Gabriel brought the good news that Mary would become mother of "the Son of the Most High" – to the house of Elizabeth in the hill country of Judah. The angel had told Mary the extraordinary news that her cousin, Elizabeth, in her old age had conceived a son "and is now in her sixth month" (Luke 1:36). Mary went immediately to be of service to her old cousin in the final months of her pregnancy. Mary's greeting of Elizabeth as she entered her house brought an extraordinary blessing to her and to the child within her womb. St Luke writes:

> Now it happened that as soon as Elizabeth heard Mary's greeting, the child leapt in her womb and Elizabeth was filled with the Holy Spirit. She gave a loud cry and said: Of all women you are the most blessed and blessed is the fruit of your womb. Why should I be honoured with a visit from the mother of my Lord? Look, the moment your greeting reached my ears, the child in my womb leapt for joy. Yes, blessed is she who believed that the promise made her by the Lord would be fulfilled. (Luke 1:41-45)

Notice that we are quoting the very words of Elizabeth when we say to Mary, "blessed are you among women". God the Father was the first to call Mary "full of grace" and now Elizabeth, filled with the Holy Spirit, proclaims that she is *blessed among women*.

Blessed Is the Fruit of Thy Womb

At the very sound of Mary's voice Elizabeth experienced her "personal Pentecost". She was "filled with the Holy Spirit"; she received the gift of faith, which enabled her to proclaim that Mary is "the mother of my Lord"; she acknowledged that the fruit of Mary's womb is blessed; the child in her own womb, John the Baptist, leapt for joy. And when her son was born and his father, Zechariah, in obedience to the word of the archangel Gabriel, called him *John*, he too "was filled with the Holy Spirit and spoke in prophecy" (Luke 1:67). Zechariah had lost his speech because he didn't believe that his wife in her old age could conceive a child. The angel said to him, "Listen! Since you have not believed my words which will come true at the appointed time, you will be silenced and have no power of speech until this has happened" (Luke 1:20). Zechariah's gift of speech is restored and he receives the gift of faith and proclaims, "Blessed be the Lord the God of Israel, for he has visited his people, he has come to their rescue and has raised up for us a power of salvation... And you little child will be called Prophet of the Most High for you will go before the Lord to prepare a way for him" (Luke 1:68-69. 76). Zechariah believed that through Mary bearing the Son of God in her womb, God had visited his people and brought all these wonderful blessings to his house.

As we pray the Hail Mary we are proclaiming our own faith in God – in God the Father who invites Mary to become the mother of the Son of God; in God the Holy Spirit through whose power Mary conceives the Son of God in her womb. Only the person who believes in God, Father, Son and the Holy Spirit, can pray the Hail Mary and assent to the meaning of the words. That is why we say the prayer is a Trinitarian prayer, a profound profession of our faith in the mystery of the Holy Trinity.

In the second part of the Hail Mary we begin by professing our faith that Mary is the Mother of God, and we ask for her prayers.

Holy Mary, Mother of God

With this greeting we now profess our faith in the great mystery of Jesus, the Son of God and the son of Mary. Today we take it for granted that Mary is the Mother of God. But that truth of our faith was not always accepted by everyone. A very early heresy in the fourth century challenged the belief that Mary is the Mother of God. Nestorius, the patriarch of Constantinople, argued that Mary was the mother of the man Jesus, but not the Mother of the Son of God. He said that Mary was mother of Christ (*Christotokos* in Greek) but not Mother of God (*Theotokos* in Greek). Eventually a General Council of the Church was held in the city of Ephesus (in modern Turkey) in AD 431 to discuss this controversy. The Council issued this decree: "If anyone does not confess that Emmanuel is truly God and therefore that the blessed Virgin is truly Mother of God (*Theotokos*), for she bore according to the flesh him who is the Word of God, let him be anathema."[54] The Church defended the unity of Christ as a person. There is only one person in Christ and that person is divine; that person is the Son of God. Mary is the mother of that person. A mother is not just the mother of her child's body. She is the mother of the person who grows in her womb, to whom she gives birth, whom she nurses, nurtures and educates. Because we believe that Mary's child was God incarnate, God become man, we acknowledge her as Mother of God. This has been the Church's great defence of the divinity of Christ. St Pope John Paul II writes:

> The dogma of the divine motherhood of Mary was for the Council of Ephesus and is for the Church like a seal upon the dogma of the Incarnation, in which the Word truly assumes human nature into the unity of his person, without cancelling out that nature.[55]

Every time we pray, "Holy Mary, Mother of God," we are professing our faith in the divinity of Jesus Christ. Only one who believes in the divinity of Christ can say the Hail Mary and assent to this great truth. Devotion to Mary has been, down through the ages, the bulwark against all heresies about the person of Jesus Christ. As we pray, "Holy Mary, Mother of God," it is helpful to linger a little on those words and let their meaning sink into the depth of our being in new ways. This is who Jesus Christ is: he is the Son of God; and this is who Mary is: she is the Mother of God.

Pray for Us Sinners

We now have a big request to make to the Mother of God, our spiritual mother. We say, "Pray for us sinners." In our prayer we have acknowledged that Mary is the woman who is *full of grace*, *kecharitomene.* Now we acknowledge, as we stand in her presence in prayer, that we are sinners. We need her prayers, and since she is our spiritual mother we believe that she is ever ready to help us. As a sign of the great ecumenical progress that is taking place among the various Christian Churches, the British Methodist-Roman Catholic Committee, in its agreed statement in 1995, was able to write:

> Motherhood is a permanent relationship. Now that Christians are incorporated into Christ, united to our Head as his Body, Mary has a maternal relation to all believers as symbolised by John: "Woman, behold your son: son, behold your mother" (John 19:26). Mary is the mother of the "whole Christ", Head and members together, but she remains at the same time a fellow disciple and our sister in God's family.[56]

Jesus Christ, the son of Mary, is our one and only mediator with God the Father. Mary is not the mediator. But Mary, by the will and word of Jesus, is the mother of all those for whom Jesus is mediating with God the Father. She is the mother of Christ, the whole Christ, head and members. That too is why we call Jesus our brother. He is our brother because by his gift on the cross Mary is our mother. How could we call Jesus our brother if we refused to call his mother our mother? And if Mary is our mother "in the order of grace", how could we refuse to ask her for the graces we need?

From the earliest days of the Church the faithful went in prayer to Mary for help in all their needs. We still say a prayer to Our Lady today that Christians as early as the third century were saying:

> We fly to thy patronage,
> O holy Mother of God.
> Despise not our petitions in our necessities,
> but deliver us from all dangers,
> O glorious and Blessed Virgin.

The earliest version of this prayer, written in Greek, dates from around AD 250. Cardinal Shönborn, commenting on this ancient prayer, writes: "The oldest versions of this prayer, written on papyrus, have a peculiar feature that is quite beautiful. They do not begin with 'We fly to thy patronage' but rather 'we fly to thy mercy, O Mother of God.'"[57]

Even as early as the third century, Christians were writing down their prayer to Our Lady and encouraging one another to fly to her mercy. Right from the beginning of the Church, the Holy Spirit inspired in the hearts of the faithful the insight of faith that showed them that they should go to the mother of Jesus and receive her protection and experience her mercy. Mary's mercy, of course, is the mercy that God gives her in abundance so that she can show his great mercy to us. She embraces us with the abundant mercy of God the Father.

We have that other wonderful prayer to Our Lady, the Memorare:

> Remember, O most gracious Virgin Mary,
> that never was it known that anyone who fled to your protection,
> implored your help, or sought your intercession,
> was left unaided.
> Inspired with this confidence,
> I fly unto you, O Virgin of virgins, my Mother.
> To you do I come, before you I stand, sinful and sorrowful.
> O Mother of the Word Incarnate,
> despise not my petitions,
> but in your mercy, hear and answer me.
> Amen

This is a very confident prayer to our Mother of Mercy. Those who say this prayer, especially in times of difficulty, experience Our Lady's swift response. The sentiments expressed in this prayer correspond to the experience of the faithful: "never was it known that anyone who fled to your protection, implored your help, or sought your intercession, was left unaided". What an extraordinary assertion of total trust in Mary's help. Notice that we are appealing to her mercy. Jesus said, "Be merciful, as your heavenly Father is merciful" (Luke 6:36). Mary lives by this word and shows to us the great mercy she herself received from the Father when she was conceived without original sin, the wonderful mercy of her immaculate conception. Now, as our Mother of Mercy, Mary yearns to share that mercy with each of us. And just as a mother gives her special care and attention to the sick child in the family, so Mary has a very special care for each of us in our own weakness, whatever it may be. It is so important for us, then, to entrust to her motherly care all our weaknesses and all our sinfulness. She is sinless and we are sinners. That is why we can confidently say to her, "Pray for us sinners."

Spiritual Motherhood

As our spiritual mother, Mary has a personal relationship with each of us. She is now body and soul in heaven and she knows each of us by name. She relates personally to each of us. You are not just one in a billion who calls on her for help. St Pope John Paul II speaks very clearly about this unique relationship that Mary our mother now has with each one of us:

> Motherhood always establishes a unique and unrepeatable relationship between two people: between mother and child and between child and mother. Even when the same mother has many children, her personal relationship with each of them is of the very essence of motherhood... It can be said that motherhood "in the order of grace" preserves the analogy with what "in the order of nature" characterizes the union between mother and child.[58]

Mary knows your name, the name you received when you were baptised and became a child of God. At that very moment you became her son or daughter too. Believing that Mary, the mother of Jesus, is also our spiritual mother fills us with great confidence, not only in our relationship with Mary, but also in our relationship with Jesus. Jesus now recognises us as his brothers and sisters. On the morning of his resurrection he said to Mary Magdalene: "Go and find the brothers and tell them: I am ascending to my Father and your Father, to my God and your God" (John 20:17).

Now

We need Mary's great motherly intercession at two moments in our life: we need it now, in this present moment, and we need it at the hour of our death. Because she is our spiritual mother, who knows each of us by name, who understands all our weaknesses, she is ever ready to help us.

Every day we are tempted to forget who we truly are as sons and daughters of God; to forget that we are always in God's presence; to forget that Jesus Christ, the Son of God, has redeemed us, given us the new life of the Spirit, and offers us fresh hope each day; to forget that we are capable of loving one another just as Jesus loves us; to forget that we are spiritual men and women, reflecting the very image and likeness of God; to forget that we have been created for everlasting life with God in heaven. Because of this forgetfulness we are very easily tempted to seek even momentary happiness, by acting in ways that are purely selfish and self-seeking. So we are easily tempted to sin. That is why we need Mother Mary's intercession each day and why we ask her to "pray for us now", in this present moment. Those who seek Our Lady's prayers are never disappointed.

At the dawn of each new day we need Our Lady's help. It is, therefore, a very good spiritual practice to pray the Hail Mary each morning, immediately after we pray the Our Father. When we ask Mother Mary to pray for us now, this very day, we believe that she takes us under her protection in a special way. And especially when we fail and fall again into sin, she will be at our side to help us to begin again, to acknowledge our sins and ask for God's mercy and forgiveness. She will remind us of her own great prayer of praise, the Magnificat, in which she says: "His mercy reaches from age to age for those who fear him... He has come to the help of Israel his servant, mindful of his mercy to Abraham and to his descendants for ever" (Luke 1:50. 54-55).

She will encourage us never to lose heart because of our sins but to confidently celebrate the great sacrament of reconciliation, when we will hear the priest say:

> God, the Father of mercies, through the death and resurrection of his Son has reconciled the world to himself and sent the Holy Spirit among us for the forgiveness of sins; through the ministry of the Church may God give you pardon and peace and I absolve you from your sins in the name of the Father, the Son and the Holy Spirit. The Lord has freed you from your sins. Go in peace.

Nothing gives Mary, the Mother of Mercy, greater joy than to see us celebrate the great forgiveness that her Son gives us when we celebrate the sacrament of reconciliation. The first thing pilgrims to the shrines of Our Lady around the world notice is the number of people queuing up to celebrate this great sacrament. In Lourdes, in Fatima, in Knock and in Medjugorje I have always been deeply impressed by the thousands of pilgrims who queue, patiently awaiting their turn to celebrate the sacrament of confession. Mother Mary always responds when we ask her to *pray for us sinners*. And her powerful prayers bring us "to the throne of grace where we find mercy and grace when we are in need of help" (Hebrews 4:16).

At the Hour of Our Death

We pray for Mary's help not just for today but also for the most important day of our life in this world, the day that God will call us home to be with him for ever in heaven. If we have asked Mary for help each day we can be absolutely certain that on our final day in this world she will come to be with us as our spiritual mother. She will comfort us in moments of doubt and fear; she will assure us that her Son Jesus Christ has redeemed us from all our sins and that we are now ready to enter into the glory of God; she will obtain for us the grace to leave this world in peace, the great and final grace in this world, the grace of a happy death.

The importance of this prayer was indelibly imprinted on my mind three years before I was ordained a priest, when I had the grace to be with my family at home, saying the Rosary around the bed of our father, as he was dying. My father had said the Rosary at home every day of his life. My earliest memory as a boy at home is of kneeling down with him and my mother, and with all my brothers and sisters (there were ten of us), saying the Rosary together. Every day of his life my father had prayed to Our Lady, "Pray for us now and at the hour of our death." And now, at the hour of his death, we were praying the third glorious mystery of the Rosary, the descent of the Holy Spirit, as he peacefully breathed his last. Years later, as a family we had the same experience as we gathered around the bed of our mother as she was dying. She had faithfully prayed the Rosary every day of her life. And now, as we were praying, reminding her that Our Lord and his mother were with her, she peacefully breathed her last. It is at moments like these that we realise more fully that no prayer ever goes unanswered, no Hail Mary is ever said in vain. Mary always hears and she never forgets.

As we pray the Hail Mary we are opening our whole life to the mystery of Christ who was born of Mary, who redeemed us through his great love and perfect obedience to his Father's will and who, as his parting gift from the cross, gave us his mother Mary to be our mother. That is why we treasure this beautiful prayer that we call the Hail Mary.

❖

— Chapter 5 —

Praying for the Gift of the Holy Spirit

The one gift that God the Father never refuses to give us, when we ask him for it in Jesus' name, is the gift of the Holy Spirit. Jesus encourages us to ask persistently for this gift:

> Ask and it will be given to you; search and you will find; knock and the door will be opened to you. For everyone who asks receives; everyone who searches finds; everyone who knocks will have the door opened. What father among you, if his son asked for a fish, would hand him a snake? Or, if he asked for an egg, hand him a scorpion? If you then, evil though you are, know how to give your children what is good, how much more will your heavenly Father give the Holy Spirit to those who ask him. (Luke 11:9-13)

The sanctifying, comforting and guiding presence of the Holy Spirit is the great gift that God the Father has for us and for which we should ask constantly in prayer. Throughout the Hebrew scriptures, the Old Testament, God promises us this gift. The prophet Joel, summing up all the promises of God, said: "I shall pour out my Spirit on all humanity. Your sons and your daughters shall prophesy, your old people shall dream dreams, and your young people see visions" (Joel 2:28). It was through Jesus, through his death and resurrection, that God fulfilled this great promise and poured forth his Holy Spirit. Jesus said to his disciples: "I will ask the Father and he will give you another Paraclete to be with you for ever, the Spirit of truth whom the world can never accept since it neither sees nor knows him; but you know him because he is with you, he is in you" (John 14:16-17).

Christ's Promise of the Spirit

Christ's disciples were upset when he told them that he would have to leave them. To comfort and reassure them he said: "You are sad at heart because I have told you this. Still, I am telling you the truth; it is for your own good that I am going, because unless I go, the Paraclete will not come to you; but if I go, I will send him to you" (John 16:6-7). Jesus is telling them that it is better for them to have the invisible presence of the Holy Spirit than to have his own visible presence. And, furthermore, he told them that they know the Spirit "because he is with you, he is in you". Jesus is speaking the same words to us: the invisible presence of the Holy Spirit is better for us than his own visible presence. He is also saying to us, "You know the Spirit, because he is with you, he is in you."

Getting to know the Holy Spirit is the spiritual quest in the heart of each believer in Christ. That is why Jesus assures us that the Father will always give the gift of the Spirit to those who ask him. Our constant prayer should be, "Come, Holy Spirit."

Without the Holy Spirit we cannot know that we are children of God. St Paul tells us: "As you are sons, God has sent into our hearts the Spirit of his Son crying, '*Abba,* Father'; and so you are no longer a slave, but a son; and if a son, then an heir, by God's own act" (Galatians 4:6-7). St Paul also says, "Nobody is able to say 'Jesus is Lord' except in the Holy Spirit" (1 Corinthians 12:3). Without this grace of the indwelling of the Holy Spirit in our hearts we cannot believe in Jesus nor can we accept the salvation that he has won for us.

It is through the grace of the Holy Spirit in our hearts that we know Jesus as our Lord and Saviour, and God as our gracious Father. This is the traditional prayer of the Church for the blessing of the Holy Spirit in our lives:

> Come Holy Spirit, fill the hearts of your faithful and kindle in them the fire of your love. Send forth your Spirit, O

Lord, and they shall be created and you shall renew the face of the earth. O God, who enlightens the hearts of the faithful by the light of the Holy Spirit, grant that by this same gift we may be always truly wise and ever rejoice your consolations, through Christ our Lord.

In Jesus the Promise of the Spirit is Fulfilled

The archangel Gabriel announced to Mary: "The Holy Spirit will come upon you and the power of the Most High will cover you with its shadow. And the child will be holy and will be called the Son of God" (Luke 1:35). The Son of God became the son of Mary through the power of the Holy Spirit and was born into this world as a human being like us in all things but sin.

Jesus entered into our human history, as our Saviour, through the power of the Holy Spirit. Everything Jesus did in the work of our salvation he did in the power of the Holy Spirit. As we saw in our reflections on the baptism of Jesus by John the Baptist in the first chapter of this book, Jesus began preaching the Gospel only after he was filled with the Holy Spirit at the time of his baptism by John.

As Jesus goes about preaching the Gospel we see him engaging in four different ministries: he is a preacher of the Good News of our salvation; he is a teacher of the new life in the kingdom of God; he is a healer of the sick who come to him for healing; he is an exorcist who drives out the evil spirits that trouble people. When the Pharisees saw his work as an exorcist they said: "This man drives out devils only through Beelzebul, the chief of the devils." Jesus replied: "If it is through Beelzebul that I drive devils out, through whom do your own experts drive them out? They shall be your judges. But if it is through the Spirit of God that I drive devils out, then know that the kingdom of God has caught you unawares" (Matthew 12:24. 27-28).

Jesus promised his disciples the very same power of the Spirit that he himself had. We read in the Acts of the Apostles: "While at table

85

with them, he had told them not to leave Jerusalem, but to wait there for what the Father had promised. 'It is,' he had said, 'what you have heard me speak about: John baptised with water but not many days from now, you are going to be baptised with the Holy Spirit... you will receive the power of the Holy Spirit which will come on you, and then you will be my witnesses not only in Jerusalem but throughout Judea and Samaria, and indeed to earth's remotest end" (Acts 1:4-5. 8).

Jesus Establishes His Church through the Holy Spirit

Jesus, as St Peter says, was anointed with the fullness of the Holy Spirit by God his Father (Acts 10:38). He came to share that Spirit, that anointing, with us. That is the gift of our salvation. Indeed, someone has aptly defined the Church in this way: "the community of those who share in the anointing of the Anointed One". The very word *Christ* means the Anointed One. Jesus cannot share with us his unique union with God whereby he and the Father are one. We call that union the "hypostatic union" – unique to Jesus and incommunicable to us. But he can communicate to us what he received from the Father – namely, his anointing with the Holy Spirit. This communication of the Spirit, this imparting of the Spirit, is the creation of the Church. He promised his disciples: "I shall ask the Father, and he will give you another Advocate to be with you for ever, that Spirit of truth whom the world cannot receive since it neither sees him nor knows him; but you know him because he is with you, he is in you" (John 14:16-17). In response to this intercession of Jesus, the Father sent the other Advocate. He poured out his Holy Spirit on the disciples. This is the mystery of Pentecost, the mystery of the Church.

The Second Vatican Council has made it very clear that the Church is established by Christ when the Spirit is poured out: "By communicating his Spirit to his brothers, called together from all people, Christ made them mystically his own body."[59] After being lifted up on the cross and glorified, the Lord Jesus poured forth the Spirit whom he had promised, and through whom he called and gathered the people of the New Covenant.[60]

The Church comes into being through Christ's intercession with the Father: "I will ask the Father and he will give you another Paraclete" (John 14:16). St John describes in detail how this gift of the other Paraclete was given:

> In the evening of that same day, the first day of the week, the doors were closed in the room where the disciples were, for fear of the Jews. Jesus came and stood among them. He said to them, "Peace be with you," and showed them his hands and his side. The disciples were filled with joy when they saw the Lord, and he said to them again, "Peace be with you. As the Father sent me, so am I sending you." After saying this he breathed on them and said: "Receive the Holy Spirit." (John 20:19-22)

Reborn of Water and the Holy Spirit

It is through the breath of Christ, breathing on us and filling us with the Holy Spirit, that we are the Church of Christ today. We become members of Christ's body, the Church, through our baptism, when, as Jesus says, "we are reborn of water and the Holy Spirit" (John 3:5). The Holy Spirit plays the central role in our rebirth. As the Catechism says:

> In the liturgy the Holy Spirit is teacher of the faith of the People of God and artisan of "God's masterpiece", the sacraments of the New Covenant. The desire and work of the Spirit in the heart of the Church is that we may live from the life of the risen Christ. When the Spirit encounters in us the response of faith which he has aroused in us, he brings about genuine co-operation. Through it, the liturgy becomes the common work of the Holy Spirit and the Church.[61]

What Difference Does the Holy Spirit Make in Our Lives?

It is very helpful and indeed very necessary for us to reflect on and become aware of this invisible, abiding presence of the Holy Spirit at work in the Church, in the world and in our hearts. The Spirit is the active memory of the Church; he is the teacher of our faith: "By his transforming power, he makes the mystery of Christ present here and now."[62] The Spirit is in the good works, the witness of Christians all over the world, as they seek to live the life of Christ; when we pray, it is the Spirit who prays in our hearts. To answer that question – *what difference does the Holy Spirit make in our lives?* – the Greek Orthodox patriarch of Syria, Ignatius IV, gave this very clear explanation in his address to the World Council of Churches:

> Without the Holy Spirit:
> God is far away,
> Christ stays in the past,
> the Gospel is a dead letter,
> the Church simply an organisation,
> authority simply a matter of domination,
> mission a matter of propaganda,
> liturgy no more than an evocation,
> Christian living a slave morality.
> But with the Holy Spirit:
> the cosmos is resurrected and groans
> with the birth-pangs of the Kingdom,
> the risen Christ is there,
> the Gospel is the power of life,
> the Church shows forth the life of the Trinity,
> authority is a liberating service,
> mission is Pentecost,
> the liturgy is both memorial and anticipation,
> human action is deified.[63]

With Bishop Ignatius' clear teaching on the difference that the Holy Spirit makes in our lives we will begin to understand more clearly what Jesus meant when he said, "It is for your own good that I am going, because unless I go, the Paraclete will not come to you; but if I go, I will send him to you" (John 16:7). We can now see how the Holy Spirit is invisibly at work in the very creation of the Church, in our own membership of the Church, in our families and in our hearts each time we turn to God in prayer. In fact, we can only turn to God in prayer because the Spirit is already in our hearts. As St Paul said:

> You, however, live not by your natural inclinations, but by the Spirit, since the Spirit of God has made a home in you. Indeed, anyone who does not have the Spirit of Christ does not belong to him. But when Christ is in you, the body is a dead thing because of sin but the spirit is alive because you have been justified; and if the Spirit of him who raised Jesus from the dead has made his home in you, then he who raised Christ Jesus from the dead will give life to your mortal bodies through the Spirit living in you. (Romans 8:9-11)

The Holy Spirit in Our Hearts

The Holy Spirit is Christ's first gift to us and he makes his home in our hearts. As we have seen, God the Father never refuses the gift of the Spirit to those who ask him. The Holy Spirit within us enables us to acknowledge all that Christ has achieved for us: we acknowledge that we have become the children of God through Christ because he teaches us to call God "Abba, Father". And when we pray in that way, "the Spirit himself joins with our spirit to bear witness that we are children of God" (Romans 8:16). Our human reason alone cannot give us the assurance that we are children of God – it can only come through the Holy Spirit. The Holy Spirit brings to our consciousness the awareness that we are God's children and prays within us. As Tom Smail wrote, we must pray this prayer *for ourselves* but we cannot pray it *by ourselves*.[64] None of us can decide simply by our own reason to accept God as our loving Father. That acceptance, that recognition, comes from the presence of the Holy Spirit in our hearts. In the same way, the Spirit also brings to our consciousness the fact that Jesus Christ is now seated at the right hand of the Father and enables us to acknowledge this mystery by proclaiming, *Jesus Christ is Lord.*

The confession of the lordship of Jesus comes through the grace of the Holy Spirit's personal presence in our hearts. We must make this profession of faith *for ourselves* but we cannot make it *by ourselves.* This profession is the work of grace. Without this grace of faith all the study in the world will not enable us to proclaim that Jesus Christ is Lord. As Tom Smail points out:

> The techniques of biblical scholarship can certainly bring us to a more accurate appreciation of what the biblical writers are saying; but, to bring us to the conviction of the truth of the Gospel and a relationship with the God of whom it speaks, is the prerogative of the Holy Spirit alone.[65]

Without the Holy Spirit, God the Father's great plan for his human family, in sending Christ to redeem us, will not be realised. Our hearts would remain closed to God. It is only when "the Spirit makes his home" in us that we become spiritually alive, full of thanksgiving to God for his great love, and grateful to Christ for redeeming us and sending us the Spirit through whom we have been "reborn" and through whom we become a "new creation" (2 Corinthians 5:17). As St Paul says to us: "Do you not realise that you are a temple of God with the Spirit of God living in you?" (1 Corinthians 3:16).

The Gifts of the Spirit

Jesus made this great promise to his disciples: "You will receive power when the Holy Spirit comes and then you will be my witnesses" (Acts 1:8). This power of the Spirit becomes operational in us through the gifts of the Spirit that we receive in our baptism and confirmation. We often call these gifts the charisms of the Holy Spirit. The Second Vatican Council gave us this clear teaching on the gifts of the Spirit:

> It is not only through the sacraments and the ministries of the Church that the Holy Spirit sanctifies and leads the people of God and enriches it with virtues, but, allotting his gifts to everyone according as He wills, He distributes special graces among the faithful of every rank.[66]

Each baptised person has received special gifts of the Holy Spirit for his or her life and mission in the world. As St Pope John Paul II said: "The powers of the Spirit, the gifts of the Spirit, and the fruits of the Holy Spirit are revealed in men and women."[67]

We are given these powers and gifts in order to become "Christ's witnesses". Pope Benedict XVI described what it means to become a witness in this way: "We become witnesses when, through our actions, words and way of being, Another makes himself present."[68]

When we live and work in the Holy Spirit we are never alone: Another – that is, Jesus – makes himself present. Jesus becomes present to those we are working with and working for. This, of course, is an invisible presence for us, but for those we are trying to help it can become quite tangible. And we don't have to be a great saint before the Holy Spirit uses us in this way. Whenever we are trying to help others in faith, Christ is always present. It is through the Holy Spirit that we are able to share our faith with others. Blessed Pope Paul VI said:

> Evangelization will never be possible without the action of the Holy Spirit... The Holy Spirit places on our lips the words which we could not find by ourselves, and at the same time the Holy Spirit predisposes the soul of the hearer to be open and receptive to the Good News and to the Kingdom being proclaimed.[69]

It is the Holy Spirit who will give you and your parish the confidence to become involved in the new evangelisation. But often the doubt lingers. Am I qualified? Is my parish qualified? Pope Francis addressed this doubt head-on when he stated:

> All the baptized, whatever their position in the Church or their level of instruction in the faith, are agents of evangelization, and it would be insufficient to envisage a plan of evangelization carried out by professionals while the rest of the faithful would remain simply passive.[70]

Each of us has received the gift of the Holy Spirit. We are qualified by the Spirit to share our faith with others, to spread the Good News that Christ has redeemed us, that he wants each person in our world, no matter what their difficulties or no matter how deaf they may seem to be to the promptings of the Spirit in their lives, to receive the gift of faith and the blessing of God our Father. The Holy Spirit wants us to share this Good News by the way we live and seek to help others. When you find yourself helping someone in need, giving a little money, for instance, to a poor person on the street who is asking for help, it is the Holy Spirit in you who is inspiring you to do this good work. You have become a witness to Christ and your very act of generosity brings Christ to that brother or sister. You may never know the good your generous act has done, but the Holy Spirit will use it for the benefit of the other person whom you have accepted as a brother or sister in Christ in need of help of some kind. When we do a good work for others it is most beneficial to remind ourselves that we did the good work through the inspiration and grace of the Holy Spirit. The more we acknowledge to ourselves the promptings of the Spirit in the good we try to do for others, the more we become aware of the fruits of the Spirit in our lives. St Paul tells us that the fruits of the Spirit are: "love, joy, peace, patience, kindness, goodness, trustfulness, gentleness and self-control" (Galatians 5:22-23).

The Answer to All the Materialism of Our Age

St Pope John Paul II, in his first encyclical letter to the Church, called us all to reflect more deeply on the gift of the Holy Spirit which makes us one with Christ and alive in Christ. He wrote:

> The present-day Church seems to repeat with ever greater fervour and with holy insistence: "Come, Holy Spirit! Come! Come!"... This appeal to the Spirit, intended precisely to obtain the Spirit, is the answer to all the "materialisms" of our age.[71]

St Pope John Paul II's teaching that the appeal to the Spirit "is the answer to all the 'materialisms' of our age" is surely a word of encouragement that we should listen to afresh each day. It is very easy to lapse into discouragement in the Church and in our society. Many things have gone wrong in our Church; great scandals have disturbed and upset the faithful of all ages; we are very aware that vocations to the priesthood and religious life have dramatically decreased; we are acutely aware that many of our young people do not join the parish community for Sunday Mass; family life is being challenged and undermined in many ways; and with so much violence in our world today, our societies have become much less peaceful and safe. Fresh encouragement is needed to face all these challenges. We can find that encouragement in those words: "the appeal to the Spirit is the answer to all the 'materialisms' of our age". We have the answer to hand. We can invoke the Holy Spirit each day to come afresh on the Church, on our families, on our society and on ourselves. The Holy Spirit, as we say in the Creed, "is the Lord, the giver of life". As we invoke the Spirit to come, he will give new life, new hope to us and to the Church. St Paul prayed this prayer for hope through the Spirit in his letter to the Romans: "May the God of hope fill you with all joy and peace in your faith, so that in the power of the Holy Spirit you may be rich in hope" (Romans 15:13).

Reborn into a Living Hope

St Peter reminds us of this great gift of hope: "Blessed be God the Father of Our Lord Jesus Christ, who in his great mercy has given us a new birth into a living hope through the resurrection of Jesus Christ from the dead" (1 Peter 1:3). It is through the Holy Spirit, "the Lord, the giver of life", that our hope remains "a living hope". Without the Holy Spirit our hope becomes a dead hope. Our life begins to lose enthusiasm and we lose the joy that Pope Francis wrote about when he said, "The joy of the Gospel fills the hearts and lives of those who encounter Jesus. Those who accept his offer of salvation are set free from sin, sorrow, inner emptiness and loneliness."[72]

Living hope is an interior, spiritual energy that enables us to reach out and lay hold of tomorrow and to declare in advance that tomorrow will be good because tomorrow will be God's gift to us. Living hope enables us to face the future with confidence because we are not facing it alone. The power of the risen Christ is in us and with us. The Holy Spirit reminds us of the promise of Christ, that "the gates of hell will never overpower the Church" (Matthew 16:18). When we look at the calamities and dreadful atrocities that happen in our world we don't sink into despondency. Rather, we engage our lifeline, our prayer, and the Holy Spirit stirs up our living hope. At each Mass, we describe our stance before God with the words of this prayer: "Deliver us, Lord, we pray, from every evil, graciously grant peace in our days, that by the help of your mercy, we may be always free from sin and safe from all distress, as we await the blessed hope and the coming of our Saviour, Jesus Christ." In the face of all the evil that seeks to triumph in our world the Holy Spirit stirs up within us that living hope and we look forward to the fulfilment of all of God's plan for our human race when Christ will come again in glory. Evil never has the last word. Living in faith, in the awareness of the Holy Spirit in our lives, enables us, as it has enabled Christians down through the ages, to remember we are pilgrims in this world on our journey to our true fatherland, which is in heaven with God.

The Seed of Living Hope

Our proclamation during Mass, "We proclaim your death, O Lord, and profess your resurrection until you come again," opens our hearts to be filled with that "living hope" which the resurrection alone can instil. In the words of St Peter's great prayer:

> Blessed be the God and Father of our Lord Jesus Christ, who in his great mercy has given us a new birth into a living hope through the resurrection of Jesus Christ from the dead and into a heritage that can never be spoilt or soiled and never fade away. (1 Peter 1:3-4)

It is with living hope in our hearts that we await the coming of Jesus Christ in glory. St Peter says, "Always have your answer ready for people who ask you the reason for the hope that you all have" (1 Peter 3:15). We calmly face our own death because we believe in eternal life and the resurrection of our bodies. Prayer is the lifeline that keeps this hope alive and fresh in our hearts. The Second Vatican Council said: "One is right in thinking that the future of humanity rests with people who are capable of providing the generations to come with reasons for living and reasons for hoping."[73] Who has better reasons for hoping than those who believe that Christ will come again in glory? But before we can give people the reason for living and hoping we have to keep that hope alive in our own hearts. The source of that hope is in our Sunday or daily Eucharist. As St Pope John Paul II said:

> The Eucharist spurs us on through history and plants a seed of living hope in our daily commitments to the work before us. Certainly the Christian vision leads to the expectation of "a new heaven" and "a new earth" (Revelation 21:1), but this increases rather than lessens *our sense of responsibility for the world today.*[74]

The Mass plants that "seed of living hope" in our hearts. Each day our prayer to the Holy Spirit waters that seed and enables it to grow and spread and bear fruit.

Invoking the Holy Spirit During Mass

It is Christ our Lord who invokes the Spirit to come on us during the Mass because he is the High Priest of each Mass. When the priest imposes his hands over our gifts of bread and wine he prays, in Christ's name, "Make holy, therefore, these gifts, we pray, by sending down your Spirit upon them like the dewfall, so that they may become for us the Body and Blood of our Lord Jesus Christ."[75] In this invocation we acknowledge that it is through the power of the Holy Spirit that our gifts of bread and wine become for us the very Body and Blood of Christ. After the Consecration we have the second invocation of the Holy Spirit on the whole community present: "Grant that we who are nourished by the Body and Blood of your Son and filled with his Holy Spirit may become one body, one spirit in Christ." And we then pray that the Holy Spirit will bestow on us this great blessing: "May he make of us an eternal offering to you."[76] We are praying that through the coming of the Holy Spirit we become one with Christ, and that our whole being, body and soul, becomes an eternal offering to God. As the Catechism says:

> In every liturgical action the Holy Spirit is sent in order to bring us into communion with Christ and so to form his Body. The Holy Spirit is like the sap of the Father's vine which bears fruit on its branches. The most intimate co-operation of the Holy Spirit and the Church is achieved in the liturgy. The Spirit, who is the Spirit of communion, abides indefectibly in the Church.[77]

As Christians we never lose heart because, even though we are aware of our own weakness and acknowledge our sinfulness, we are much more aware that the Spirit of God has made his home in our hearts and that what we cannot do by ourselves we can do through the power and the inspiration of the Holy Spirit, the Lord, the giver of life, who abides in us. As we pray during Mass for the Holy Spirit to make us "one body, one spirit in Christ" we believe that God hears our prayer and fills us afresh with the grace and the gifts of the Holy Spirit. But as the Holy Spirit always patiently awaits our permission before he releases all the powers and graces of his gifts in our lives, we should always consciously say *yes* to what the Spirit wants to do. In the words of the well-known hymn to the Holy Spirit, we can pray: "Come take possession of our souls and make them all thine own."

The Church sums up the work of the Spirit in our lives in the Fourth Eucharistic Prayer of the Mass: "And that we might live no longer for ourselves but for him who died and rose again for us, he sent the Holy Spirit from you, Father, as the first fruits for those who believe, so that, bringing to perfection his work in the world, he might sanctify creation to the full." When we ask God the Father to fill us afresh with the Holy Spirit, as Christ encourages us to do, we always receive a new blessing of the Spirit's presence in our hearts.

Baptism in the Spirit: a new grace of renewal

We become members of the Church, members of the body of Christ, and our bodies become the temple of the Holy Spirit through the sacrament of baptism. In that great sacrament we are, as Jesus says, "born through water and the Holy Spirit" (John 3:5). We become children of God and heirs of the kingdom of God. We receive both faith and the gifts of the Spirit through the sacrament of our baptism. It has, however, been the experience of many people that these gifts, instead of making them enthusiastic for spreading the faith and the Good News of Christ, remain cold and even dormant. They know in their hearts that they want to be faithful to God, want to serve God, but somehow zeal and enthusiasm evade them. They say their prayers, but often without conviction; they go to Mass, but often just out of duty. The God in whom they believe, and whom they want to serve, seems far away. And very often Christ seems to be someone in the past. Intuitively they know that their faith is a great gift of God and they often experience a deep yearning in their hearts for a more personal relationship with God. But how can they get that relationship? What can set their faith on fire? They are really experiencing a yearning for a deeper relationship with God, a living relationship with Jesus and a true friendship with the Holy Spirit. It is the Holy Spirit who is stirring up that yearning in their hearts.

In the past fifty years, ever since the Second Vatican Council, millions of men and women have been experiencing a great release in their spirits through the ministry of their Christian brothers and sisters. They ask to be prayed with for a fresh infilling with the Holy Spirit. And God, who is always faithful to his promise, fills their hearts with great grace and gifts of the Spirit. This experience is often called "baptism in the Spirit" or "release in the Spirit". Their spirits come alive in new ways; they receive a new sense of God as their loving Father; they experience a more personal relationship with Jesus as their Lord and Saviour; they develop a deeper and more joyful awareness that they are the temple of the Holy Spirit who lives and works in them; they become hungry for the word of God and begin to read the scriptures with new eyes; prayer, especially the great prayer of the Mass, ceases to be just a duty and becomes the source of great joy and peace; they joyfully bring all their sins, failures, hurts and inner wounds to the Lord in the sacrament of reconciliation and experience deep healing as well as forgiveness; they become witnesses to Christ present in their family, in their parish and in the world. This is a powerful and often life-changing grace, one which each of us should humbly seek from the Lord each day. We can pray for this grace in our own words, asking Christ to fill us with his Holy Spirit and give us all the gifts of the Spirit that we need. Or you might find the following kind of prayer helpful because I have focused each part of it on some special gift that we are asking from Our Lord:

> Lord Jesus Christ, I accept you as my Lord, my Saviour and my King. I invite you to come afresh into my heart, forgive me all my sin and heal every wound of sin. Baptise me in your Holy Spirit; release within me all the gifts of

the Spirit that I received in my baptism; fill me with your love and your peace because I want to be your faithful disciple in the world.

In his very short Epistle, St Jude says this to us: "But you, my dear friends, must build yourselves up on the foundation of your most holy faith, praying in the Holy Spirit" (Jude 1:20). That is how to pray. And when you feel that you do not know how to pray, St Paul encourages you with these words: "The Spirit comes to help us in our weakness for when we do not know how to pray properly, then the Spirit personally makes our petitions for us in groans that cannot be put into words" (Romans 8:26).

Right now, as you come to the end of this chapter, you can invoke the Holy Spirit to come and renew within you all the graces and gifts that he gave you on the day of your baptism and ask for the grace to pray always in the Spirit. There are others in your parish who will have the same yearning in their hearts as you have in yours to "pray in the Holy Spirit". If you know a few, why not invite them to consider sharing a time of prayer with you, in your home or in theirs, once a week? That is how new spiritual movements in our Church always begin. As Jesus says, "Where two or three meet in my name, I shall be there with them" (Matthew 18:20). Because the Lord Jesus will be with you, when two or three of you meet in his name, you will need no other teacher. As you pray together for the outpouring of the Holy Spirit on your families, on the Church, on the world and on yourselves, you will be guided in every step you take and you will receive from the Spirit the light and the wisdom you need.

❖

— Chapter 6 —

The Mass: our great Eucharistic prayer

We have, as we have seen, beautiful prayers like the Lord's Prayer and the Hail Mary which we say very frequently, perhaps several times a day. But we have also the great community prayer that we say each time we gather for the celebration of the Holy Mass. That is our great Eucharistic prayer. Joining in the celebration of Holy Mass is our most privileged time of prayer. It is also a time for which we should prepare well. The Second Vatican Council emphasised this preparation: "But in order that the liturgy may be able to produce its full effects it is necessary that the faithful come to it with proper dispositions, that their minds be attuned to their voices, and that they cooperate with heavenly grace lest they receive it in vain."[78]

It helps our prayerful participation in the Mass to take a fresh look, from time to time, at the various parts of the Mass and keep reminding ourselves of the structure of this great community prayer.

The Structure of Our Eucharistic Prayer

We gather together as a community of faith; we acknowledge our sinfulness and ask for pardon from God; we listen to God's word and we respond; we also listen to the preacher reflecting on the word; we pray for the whole Church throughout the world and for all the intentions of the gathered community; we bring our gifts of bread and wine to the altar and the priest offers them to God; then the priest prays for the Holy Spirit to come upon our gifts and transform them into the very Body and Blood of Christ; we next pray for the Holy Spirit to come on all of us gathered together so that "we may become one body, one spirit in Christ"; we then receive Holy Communion; we become the Eucharist we celebrate; we are sent forth, at the end of Mass, to bring the Good News of Christ to others.

We are involved in many different prayer movements during the Mass. We try to be fully aware of each movement and consciously enter into it. The Second Vatican Council, which sought to renew the way in which we celebrate all the sacraments, and especially the Mass, said:

> The Church spares no effort in trying to ensure that, when present at this mystery of faith, Christian believers should not be there as strangers or silent spectators. On the contrary, having a good grasp of it through the rites and prayers, they should take part in the sacred action, actively, fully aware, and devoutly. They should be formed by God's word, and nourished at the table of the Lord's Body. They should give thanks to God. Offering the immaculate victim, not only through the hands of the priest but also together with him, they should learn to offer themselves.[79]

We are not present at Mass as spectators or as private individuals saying our own prayers. We are participating "in the sacred action, actively, fully aware, and devoutly". To help ourselves to enter more fully into the sacred action of our Sunday Mass it is very helpful to keep in mind all the various movements that we engage in as we move through this great time of prayer. We will look at each movement of prayer separately.[80]

We Gather

We gather together as a community of faith to celebrate our Sunday Mass. This gathering, this coming together as the congregation, is the Church assembled. The assembly of the faithful, not the building in which they assemble, is the original meaning of the word "church". As we gather in his name, the Lord Jesus Christ himself is present in our midst. He assures us: "Where two or three meet in my name, I am there among them" (Matthew 18:20). Jesus is already waiting for us as we join our assembled brothers and sisters on the Sunday morning.

We acknowledge his presence. We are now on holy ground. We are in the presence of Jesus in the Blessed Sacrament in the tabernacle, but we are also in the presence of Jesus in the congregation that is gathering. Our full and conscious participation in the prayer of the Mass requires that we become still within ourselves at this moment, reverently acknowledging neighbours and friends, but not treating the time of waiting for the "Mass to begin" as if we were in the marketplace, catching up on the news. *Talk to God before the Mass, to your neighbour after the Mass* is a good guide. Becoming aware of where we are as we join the congregation gathering for the celebration of Mass is the first prayer movement we have to engage in. We remind ourselves that we are on holy ground and we say to ourselves, "Christ is here; he is with me and with each person who is coming into the church for Mass." Entering your heart and remaining still, even if others around you are talking, is a necessary preparation of mind and heart for the fully conscious celebration of the Mass. The great celebration of the Mass, then, begins even before the priest comes to the altar. The faithful are gathering with their hearts lifted up to the Lord.

We Confess Our Sins

When the priest arrives at the altar to begin the Mass he greets us all with the following beautiful words: *The grace of our Lord Jesus Christ, and the love of God, and the communion of the Holy Spirit, be with you all*; he may also choose the greeting, *Grace to you and peace from God our Father and the Lord Jesus Christ*; or he may use the shorter greeting, *The Lord be with you.* He then invites us to remember that even though we are now in God's holy presence we need his forgiveness. He says to us: *Brothers and sisters, let us acknowledge our sins and so prepare ourselves to celebrate the sacred mysteries.* This is a moment of interiority, the moment in which we enter our hearts, where we are alone with God and in his presence acknowledge that we need his forgiveness. It is not a moment to make us miserable but the moment in which we celebrate God's great mercy and forgiveness. It is the moment in which we place all our trust in God. St John encourages us with these words of the Lord: "If we say we have no sin, we are deceiving ourselves, and the truth has no place in us; if we acknowledge our sins, he is trustworthy and upright, so that he will forgive our sins and will cleanse us from all evil" (1 John 1:8-9). This invitation to acknowledge our sins and ask for forgiveness is a moment of great grace, the cleansing, purifying and healing grace of the Holy Spirit. We acknowledge that we are sinners not only to God but also to one another. We say together as a community, *I confess to almighty God and to you my brothers and sisters that I have greatly sinned, in my thoughts and in my words, in what I have done and in what I have failed to do, through my fault, through my fault, through my most grievous fault.* This is a very liberating confession. We are not in denial about our own sinfulness. But notice too, we are not depressed or ashamed before one another, nor are we living in fear, because we then say, *Therefore I ask blessed Mary ever-Virgin, all the Angels and Saints, and you, my brothers and sisters, to pray for me to the Lord our God.* This public confession of our sinfulness, before one another, frees us from sitting in judgement on others, from thinking that we are better than others, and opens our hearts to feeling compassion for those who seem to go astray or lose their way in life. We are acknowledging to one another that we are all sinners and that all other sinners will be safe if they join our assembly, our community of faith. Then the priest prays this great prayer of absolution for all of us: *May almighty God have mercy on us, forgive us our sins, and bring us to everlasting life.*[81]

We Listen and We Respond

Our Mass is a sacred meal that we share with Jesus. It is a sacred banquet and Jesus himself is the host who welcomes each of us as we gather to share his banquet, his "Last Supper". The Church today uses the image of two tables to help us reflect on the nature of our Mass: the table of the word of God and the table of the Body of the Lord. Pope Benedict XVI said:

> From the two tables of the word of God and the Body of Christ, the Church receives and gives to the faithful the bread of life. Consequently it must constantly be kept in mind that the word of God, read and proclaimed in the Church in the liturgy, leads to the Eucharist as to its own connatural end.[82]

Jesus, the host of this sacred banquet, is present as we gather and he shows us to our place at the table of the word of God. Now God our Father comes to speak to us as the scriptures are being proclaimed. The Second Vatican Council says: "In the sacred books the Father who is in heaven comes lovingly to meet his children and talks with them."[83] At the table of the word of God during Mass we have a sacred moment to hear what God the Father is saying to us. This requires an effort on our part. First of all we have to give our full attention to the proclamation of the word. Our thoughts, of course, can be elsewhere as the reader begins. We have to challenge our lack of attention. God is coming to speak to us and we want to cling to every word. We try to cultivate that hunger for the word of God that the prophet Jeremiah had when he said, "When your words came, I devoured them; your word was my delight and the joy of my heart" (Jeremiah 15:16). Do we listen at the table of the word of God in a way which enables us to be nourished by what God is saying to us? If we don't listen in faith, in the awareness that God the Father is speaking to us, we will not be able to receive the word of God as "our delight and the joy of our heart". That is why it is so helpful to develop the habit of praying for the Holy Spirit to enlighten us as the reader makes his or her way to the ambo or the pulpit to proclaim the word. We could pray in the words of the young Samuel, "Speak Lord, your servant is listening" (1 Samuel 3:10), or we could simply say, "Holy Spirit enlighten my mind and heart as

I listen to the Holy Scriptures being proclaimed." God is speaking to us as the scriptures are being proclaimed, but if we do not allow the Holy Spirit to open our ear, we will not hear. The prophet Isaiah said: "Morning by morning he makes my ear alert to listen like a disciple. The Lord has opened my ear" (Isaiah 50:4-5). That is the grace we need as we listen to the Sunday readings at Mass.

There is a very close correspondence between the action of the Holy Spirit at the consecration of the bread and wine and the hearing of the word of God. Alexander Schmemann, the great Greek Orthodox theologian, wrote: "Like the consecration of the gifts, *understanding and acceptance* of the word depend not on us, not only on our desires, but above all on the sacramental transformation of the 'eyes of our mind', on the coming of the Holy Spirit."[84]

Listening in Faith

St Jerome said, "We cannot come to an understanding of Scripture without the assistance of the Holy Spirit who inspired it."[85] As we allow the Holy Spirit to open our hearts we will begin to hear the words of scripture in a new way. Scripture tells us that "the word of God is something alive and active: it cuts more incisively than any two-edged sword" (Hebrews 4:12). It is not a word from the past, about some situation in the past. It is spoken to us in the present and it sheds a searching light on our lives, both as individuals and as a community. It is spoken for our encouragement. But without faith we will not be able to hear it as a personal word. Invoking the Holy Spirit to enlighten our minds as we listen to the scripture being proclaimed is the necessary preparation for hearing the word of God. Each Sunday we should resolve to listen in faith as we sit at the table of the word of God so that we will hear what God is saying to us.

Responding with Joy

When someone speaks to us, the polite thing to do is to respond. God speaks to us as we sit at the table of the word of God during Mass and we respond. As the reader finishes the reading, he or she says, *The word of the Lord* and we all respond, *Thanks be to God*. We put our heart into our thanks. God has spoken to us and we are grateful. We are then led through a series of responses. A psalm is proclaimed and we are invited to respond at the end of each verse. For instance, on the 14th Sunday of Ordinary Time, the First Reading was from the prophet Isaiah and the responsorial psalm was Psalm 65. At the end of each verse we were invited to respond with this acclamation: *Cry out with joy to God, all the earth*. It was a response of joy and gratitude to God for speaking to us and bringing good news to us. We should be able to hear that joy and gratitude in the responses.

Each invitation to respond, throughout the Mass, is a good reminder that we are at the table of the word of God. For instance, when the priest begins the prayer of the Preface he says to us, *Lift up your hearts* and in response we say, *We lift them up to the Lord*. We try to make that response with great confidence. Our hearts, we say, are now lifted up and we will keep them lifted up to the Lord, not just during the rest of the Mass, but also during the rest of the week.

The Homily

God speaks to us at the table of the word of God, not just through the holy scriptures but also through the homily that the priest or deacon preaches. We try and listen to it in faith, asking the Holy Spirit to let the words of the preacher speak in our hearts. Pope Francis gives us a helpful description of the purpose of the homily:

> The homily cannot be a form of entertainment like those presented by the media, yet it does need to give life and meaning to the celebration. It is a distinctive genre, since it is preaching situated within the framework of a liturgical celebration; hence it should be brief and avoid the semblance of a speech or a lecture.[86]

I met an old school friend years after he had been ordained a priest and we were sharing about our experience of priestly ministry. He said that he loved every aspect of his life and ministry as a priest except one: preaching terrified him. It is worth remembering this when we have to listen to a priest who doesn't seem happy or confident about what he is saying in his homily. It is also worth reminding ourselves that just as the words of scripture will not speak to us without the grace of the Holy Spirit, so too the words of the homilist, even if he is a brilliant preacher, will not touch us without the grace of the Holy Spirit. Pope Francis explains why:

> When preaching takes place within the context of the liturgy, it is part of the offering made to the Father and a mediation of the grace which Christ pours out during the celebration. This context demands that preaching should guide the assembly, and the preacher, to a life-changing communion with Christ in the Eucharist.[87]

As we listen in faith to the word of God proclaimed in the scriptures and as we listen in faith to the preacher applying that word to our present situation, the Holy Spirit has the freedom to touch our minds and hearts with a deeper understanding.

We Offer Our Gifts

We now move from the table of the word of God to the table of the Body of the Lord. As we move, we bring our gifts to the altar, simple gifts of bread and wine which the priest offers on our behalf to God. This is a profound, symbolic movement in our Eucharistic prayer and we should always try to be fully aware of what we are doing. We are giving God a gift, not just of bread and wine, but the gift of ourselves, which the bread and wine symbolise.

The Symbolism of the Gift

When you give a friend a gift, the gift always symbolises yourself, your love for your friend. There is a new dynamic created in the very act of gift-giving. You are the *giver* of the gift; your friend becomes the *thanks-giver* to you, not just for the material gift, but for the symbol of your love which the gift represents. That manifestation of true love through your gift brings peace and joy to your friend. The same dynamic is at work when we give God our gift. We are the *giver* of the gift and God becomes *thanks-giver* to us for our gift. The bread and wine that we offer to God is received gratefully by God because it is the symbol of our love for him, the sign that we are now making a gift of ourselves to him in love and thanksgiving. The bread and wine represent "all that is within me" (Psalm 103:1) – all the good and all the bad – all the light and all the darkness – all the virtue and all the vice – our whole being.

The Offertory of the Mass is the time when we joyfully offer our whole being to God: our family and our loved ones; our joys and our successes; our sorrows and our failures. The Offertory can be a time of deep inner healing: all our hurts and our inner wounds, our disappointments and our frustrations, our family upsets and our struggles with colleagues at work, our grief at the death of a loved one or the pain of a marriage break-up, all these fabrics of our lives we offer to God. And as we confidently place our whole being in God's hands we experience his healing love and peace.

At this stage of bringing our gifts to the altar it is important for us not to exclude any part of our lives, no matter how sinful something may have been. We offer to God everything about us. God knows everything and he invites us to offer him everything, lovingly and trustingly. And as we offer everything in our whole life, good or bad, to God, we then let go of all our worries. St Peter says to us, "Unload all your burden on to him, since he is concerned for you" (1 Peter 5:7).

Let Your Spirit Come on Our Gifts

The priest, acting now in the very person of Christ, imposes his hands over our gifts on the altar and prays: *Make holy, therefore, these gifts, we pray, by sending down your Spirit upon them like the dewfall, so that they may become for us the Body and Blood of our Lord Jesus Christ.*[88] The priest is making an extraordinary request. He is asking God to transform the very bread and wine that represent us and everything about us into the Body and Blood of Our Lord Jesus Christ. He is doing what Jesus told the disciples to do at the Last Supper. St Paul's first letter to the Corinthians, written about thirty-five years after the Last Supper, gives us the first written account of the celebration of the Eucharist among the first disciples of Jesus. St Paul wrote this letter to correct some abuses that had developed in the Corinthian community. He says:

> For the tradition I received from the Lord and also handed on to you is that on the night he was betrayed, the Lord Jesus took some bread, and after he had given thanks, he broke it, and he said, "This is my body, which is for you; do this in remembrance of me." And in the same way with the cup after supper, saying, "This cup is the new covenant in my blood. Whenever you drink it, do this as a memorial of me." Whenever you eat this bread, then, and drink this cup, you are proclaiming the Lord's death until he comes. (1 Corinthians 11:23-26)

The Church has been doing what Jesus told us to do in remembrance of him since the very beginning. When we gather for Mass we are making the same offering that the first Christians made and, in return, we receive from God the same blessing that they did, we receive the very Body and Blood of Christ.

Writing about why Jesus chose to leave us the Eucharist, St Pope John Paul II said:

When the Church celebrates the Eucharist, the memorial of her Lord's death and resurrection, this central event of salvation becomes really present and "the work of our redemption is carried out". This sacrifice is so decisive for the salvation of the human race that Jesus Christ offered it and returned to the Father only *after he had left us a means of sharing in it* as if we had been present there.[89]

Jesus didn't return to the Father until he had left us the opportunity of sharing in his great sacrifice for our salvation "as if we had been present there"! Every Sunday, as we gather for Mass, we are in fact spiritually present at the table of the Lord on the night before he suffered and gave us the great gift of his Body and Blood. It is Jesus himself, through the priest, who says to us, "Take and eat, this is my Body; take and drink, this is my Blood."

The Invocation of the Spirit on the Whole Congregation

Through the coming of the Holy Spirit on our gifts at the Consecration, the bread and wine are transformed into the Body and Blood of Christ. The priest announces this transformation by proclaiming, *The mystery of faith*, to which the whole community responds, *When we eat this Bread and drink this Cup we proclaim your death, O Lord, until you come again.*[90] But notice precisely what the mystery of faith is: the bread and wine, our gifts, that represent us and everything about us, have now been transformed by the Spirit of God into the Body and Blood of Christ, and we too, by that same Holy Spirit, have been so spiritually transformed that "we become one body, one spirit in Christ". After the Consecration we have the second invocation of the Holy Spirit on the whole community present: *Grant that we who are nourished by the Body and Blood of your Son and filled with his Holy Spirit may become one body, one spirit in Christ.*[91]

This is a bold and courageous prayer for our own spiritual transformation, through the Holy Spirit, into the very Body of Christ. We pray to be changed in mind and heart, in all our attitudes towards one another and in our way of behaving in all our relationships. This transformation always depends on our own willingness to undergo our daily conversion to the Lord. We are saying that we are now open to receive this transformation. We pray for a fresh outpouring of the Holy Spirit on ourselves and everyone we brought to Mass in our hearts. This is truly a profound mystery of faith. Although we are sinners, we now pray that the Holy Spirit transform us as a community into the mystical body of Christ in the world. As St Paul says, "Now Christ's body is yourselves, each of you with a part to play in the whole" (1 Corinthians 12:27).

The mystery of faith is twofold. The bread and wine are changed into the Body and Blood of Christ, and we too are transformed and become "one body, one Spirit in Christ". The body of Christ becomes truly present under the appearance of the bread and wine on the altar and, at the same time, the body of Christ becomes mystically present in us, the community, around the altar. That is the profound mystery of our faith involving both Christ and us.

I know from my own experience that it is very easy to be distracted even at the most solemn moments of the Mass. But we should always try to be fully attentive during these great invocations of the Holy Spirit, first of all on our gifts, at the Consecration, and then on ourselves. But even if our thoughts wander, our hearts remain open to receive the Spirit and we become one body, one spirit in Christ. That is why we are celebrating the Mass. We no longer see "going to Mass" as a duty imposed on us because we are Catholics; instead, we see it as our most profound spiritual need, because we want to become one body, one spirit in Christ.

We Prepare to Receive Holy Communion

Before we approach the altar to receive Holy Communion, the priest, holding up the sacrament of the Body and Blood of Christ, proclaims: *Through him, and with him and in him, O God, almighty Father, in the unity of the Holy Spirit, all glory and honour is yours, for ever and ever.* In this prayer, known technically as the Doxology, we are offering Christ and also ourselves to the Father. St Augustine said: "If you are the body and members of Christ, then it is your sacrament that is placed on the table of the Lord; it is your sacrament that you receive."[92] We have become the body of Christ which we are now offering to God our Father. Together, as the body of Christ, the whole congregation responds to the priest's proclamation with a loud *Amen*. This is known as "the great Amen". With this ancient Hebrew word we are saying our *Yes* to what the priest has just said; *Yes* to the offering of ourselves to God; *Yes* to the mystery that here and now we stand with Christ in God's presence as the body of Christ; *Yes* to the wonderful truth that through Christ we offer the almighty Father all glory and honour. We can give no greater honour to God than what we are giving to him at that very moment. So we should put our hearts into shouting out our *Amen*.

We now prepare ourselves to receive Holy Communion. We pray together the Lord's Prayer. In this great prayer we acknowledge that all of us present, and indeed all those in our lives, belong to the family of God, and we are now coming to the Father of us all to give him honour and to ask for all the graces and help we need. The priest then re-emphasises our request by praying that God deliver us from all evil in this great prayer of deliverance: *Deliver us, Lord, we pray from every evil, graciously grant peace in our days, that by the help of your mercy, we may be always free from sin and safe from all distress, as we await the blessed hope and the coming of our Saviour, Jesus Christ.*

In that prayer we are asking for great graces: deliverance from evil of all kinds, freedom from sin and protection from all distress. Now the priest prays for a special gift of peace for our hearts in this prayer that we should ponder deeply: *Lord Jesus Christ, who said to your Apostles: "Peace I leave you, my peace I give you," look not on our sins, but on the faith of your Church, and graciously grant her peace and unity in accordance with your will.*

Christ wants us to have in our hearts the peace that he came to give us. But we have to open our hearts to receive his great peace. And the sign that we have opened our hearts is that we are now able and willing to share that peace with everyone in our lives. It is important to remember that we share this sign of peace not just with those who are physically close to us in the pews, but with those who are emotionally close to us, even though they may be many miles away. Because we have prayed to become "one body, one spirit in Christ" we offer this sign of peace to anyone who may be an enemy or who may have upset us or offended us. This is the moment of grace in which we can let go of all resentments and unforgiveness.

Behold the Lamb of God

Just before we approach the altar to receive Holy Communion the priest holds up the Body and Blood of Christ and says, *Behold the Lamb of God, behold him who takes away the sins of the world*, and we respond, *Lord I am not worthy that you should enter under my roof but only say the word and my soul shall be healed.* We are now spiritually prepared to receive Our Lord in Holy Communion. We have asked him to "to say the word", the forgiving, healing word that frees us from all our sins and heals all the wounds of our sins.

Receiving and Being Received

As we come forward to receive Holy Communion at Mass we may sometimes forget that, in the words of St Pope John Paul II: *"Each of us receives Christ*, but also *Christ receives each of us."*[93]

113

Christ received us from the moment we entered the sacred assembly to celebrate the Mass. He was there to meet us and welcome us. He invited us to take our place at the table of the word of God and spoke to us as the scriptures were being proclaimed. He invited us to "take and eat". Now, in Holy Communion, Jesus takes us, all of us, including those we may individually have problems with, into his heart in a very personal and intimate way, making us all one with him. This is the moment when we do what he asked us to do when he said, "Take and eat, this is my body, and take and drink, this is my blood." In fact, it was for this moment that the Lord came into the world. He said to his apostles and he says to us, "I have earnestly desired to eat this Passover with you before I suffer" (Luke 22:15). This is the hour when he fulfils the mission the Father gave him when he sent him into the world: "I have come that they may have life and have it to the full" (John 10:10).

For this fullness of life we need the "bread of life". Jesus says, "It is my Father who gives you the bread from heaven, the true bread; for the bread of God is that which comes down from heaven and gives life to the world" (John 6:32-33). As we come forward to receive Holy Communion it is the Father who gives us "the bread from heaven", Jesus, who is "the bread of life", and it is Jesus himself who receives us into his divine life with the Father. We should take time to ponder deeply this amazing truth that, as we come to the altar to receive Holy Communion, it is God the Father who is giving us the new "manna from heaven", "the bread of life" that is Jesus, the Lamb of God, and our paschal sacrifice.

Jesus says to us, "Abide in me, and I in you" (John 15:4). Holy Communion is the sacred moment when we abide in Christ and Christ abides in us in such an intimate and personal way that he becomes "the bread of life" that gives us his own divine life.

We Become the Eucharist We Celebrate

Christ enters our hearts in Holy Communion to so transform us that we become his body in this world. In the words of St Pope Leo the Great, "Our partaking of the Body and Blood of Christ tends only to make us become what we eat."[94] The living bread that we eat in Holy Communion is not transformed into our body; rather, we are transformed into Christ's body. St Augustine expressed this amazing truth in this way: "He who suffered for us has entrusted to us in this Sacrament his Body and Blood, which indeed he has even made us. For we have been made his Body, and by his mercy, we are that which we receive."[95]

Our Holy Communion, therefore, is much more than receiving Christ into our hearts, wonderful though that is. It is Christ receiving us so completely into his heart that we become one Spirit with him. Each time we receive Holy Communion we become more deeply one with Christ.

The Mass is the glorious mystery of our faith, the faith which enables us to believe and proclaim that Jesus Christ, the Lamb of God who takes away the sins of the world, becomes present on our altars, under the appearance of bread and wine, so that he can become for us the "bread of life". In our Holy Communion we eat the body of Christ and we become the body of Christ. We become the Eucharist we celebrate. The Eucharist is truly our greatest prayer. It is Christ's amazing gift to us. We always seek to celebrate it with that devotion that St Pope John Paul II called "Eucharistic amazement".[96]

Appendix to Chapter 6

Devotion to the Blessed Sacrament in the Tabernacle

Eucharistic amazement does not cease with the final blessing of the Mass when the priest or deacon says "Go forth, the Mass is ended" or "Go and announce the Gospel of the Lord" or simply "Go in peace". Eucharistic amazement leads us to Eucharistic adoration whenever we get the opportunity. During the past thousand years, our Catholic faith in the true presence of Christ in the Blessed Sacrament reserved in the tabernacles on the altars of our churches has inspired the faithful to make "visits to the Blessed Sacrament" in their church whenever possible. As we enter a church and see that little red sanctuary light, we know that Christ is truly present in the tabernacle. We genuflect in reference and we kneel in a prayer of adoration. St Alphonsus de Liguori, like all our great saints, had a wonderful reverence for the Blessed Sacrament and encouraged all the faithful to make a visit to their church and pray before the tabernacle because the Lord was waiting for them. In one of his most influential little books, called *Visits to the Blessed Sacrament and the Blessed Virgin Mary*, he gives us a special reflection and a prayer to Jesus in the Blessed Sacrament for each day of the month, but he asks us always to begin each visit with the following prayer:

> My Lord Jesus Christ, I believe that you are really here in this sacrament. Night and day you remain here compassionate and loving. You call, you wait for, you welcome, everyone who comes to visit you... I am before you today to do three things: to thank you for these precious gifts, to make up for all the disrespect your receive in this sacrament from those who offend you, to adore you everywhere in the world where you are present in this living bread but are left abandoned and unloved.[97]

For the first day of the month he encourages us with these words:

> Behold the source of every good, Jesus in the most Blessed Sacrament, who says, If any man thirsts let him come to me (John 7:37). Oh, what torrents of grace have the saints drawn from the fountain of the Most Blessed Sacrament for here Jesus dispenses all the merits of his Passion.

Two hundred years before the Second Vatican Council proclaimed the Universal Call to Holiness, St Alphonsus, by his preaching and his writing, was insisting that all the faithful, each according to his or her state in life, are called to holiness. And, for him, one of the great sources of this holiness was found in frequent prayer before the Blessed Sacrament in the tabernacle.

Today there has been a great revival of devotion to the Blessed Sacrament in many parishes around the world. Some parishes have "perpetual adoration", with exposition of the Blessed Sacrament even throughout the night. Parishioners sign up to "do their hour" of adoration. Other parishes have exposition of the Blessed Sacrament for a number of hours each day, while others have exposition for a few hours one day a week. If you find yourself in a parish that has this devotion to the Blessed Sacrament you will have the opportunity of "making a visit" from time to time and bringing before the Lord all your family and loved ones. If your own parish doesn't have exposition of the Blessed Sacrament, it is quite possible that a church not too far away from you has a time of exposition. You might have the opportunity from time to time to make a special visit to that church and spend some time in adoration before the Blessed Sacrament exposed. In this way, your Eucharistic amazement will deepen and remain always fresh through your Eucharistic adoration.

Chapter 7

Praying the Rosary

Praying the Rosary has been the "bread and butter" of the prayer life of many generations of Catholics for the past eight hundred years. No other form of prayer in the western Church has been more widely used or more consistently encouraged by the Church than the Rosary. Down through the centuries, men and women have found in the Rosary a true lifeline through which they have been able to breathe in the pure oxygen of prayer. The genius of the Rosary is that it can be prayed by all the faithful, educated or uneducated, young or old. It can be prayed in thanksgiving to God for help received or it can be prayed in times of trouble and desolation as a great prayer of intercession, to ask for God's protection and help. In a personal testimony to the place of the Rosary in his long life, St Pope John Paul II wrote: "From my youthful years this prayer has held an important place in my spiritual life. The Rosary has accompanied me in moments of joy and in moments of difficulty. To it I have entrusted any number of concerns; in it I have always found comfort."[98]

The Origin of the Rosary

Before we consider this great prayer in more detail, I want to mention just a few facts about its origin and its contribution to the welfare of the Church. According to tradition, St Dominic was given the Rosary by Our Lady herself, around the year 1208, and she told him to teach the people this prayer as their great defence against the heresy of Albigensianism. This was the revival of a dangerous dualism that considered the human soul as good and the body as evil. St Dominic founded the Dominican Order to preach the Gospel afresh to the people and to revive their faith. Teaching people to pray the mysteries of the Rosary, helping them to meditate on the mysteries of the Son of God becoming man, his death on the cross and his resurrection from the dead, became the most effective means of teaching the great truths of the Gospel. They were meditating on the mysteries of our redemption in Christ and our rebirth as sons and daughters of God through the outpouring of the Holy Spirit. According to tradition, it was the preaching of the Rosary that made the difference in the defence of the Christian faith against this dangerous and destructive heresy of Albigensianism.

Feast of Our Lady of the Rosary

The Rosary also played a providential role in the defence of the Church and of Christian civilisation in Europe when there was a very serious threat of invasion by the mighty Turks of the Islamic Ottoman Empire in the sixteenth century. The feast of the Holy Rosary, which the Church celebrates on 7 October each year, was instituted by St Pope Pius V, a Dominican, in thanksgiving for the naval victory that a coalition of Christian states had against the invading forces of the mighty Turkish fleet in 1571. St Pius had encouraged all of Catholic Europe to pray the Rosary while invoking the intercession of Our Lady Help of Christians for the protection of Europe, and he himself led the faithful in Rome in the recitation of the Rosary. The sailors and soldiers on the 200 Christian warships prayed the Rosary as they went into battle against the superior force of the Ottoman fleet's 300 warships. While that very significant sea battle was taking place on 7 October 1571, the faithful in Rome and in many other towns and cities were holding processions, praying the Rosary for Our Lady's protection. The fleets engaged in battle in the Gulf of Lepanto, off the west coast of Greece. Only 13 ships of the 300-strong Turkish fleet escaped from the battle. Europe was saved from what would have been a catastrophic invasion, in which great harm would have been inflicted on the Church, with Christian civilisation destroyed. St Pope Pius V attributed the victory to Our Lady's protection and he asked for the Church to celebrate the feast of Our Lady of the Rosary each year. The invocation Our Lady Help of Christians was added to the Litany of Loreto. The historic significance for the whole of Europe, and, of course, for the Church, of that victory at Lepanto can never be overstated.

The Contemplative Dimension of the Rosary

Devotion to Mary always leads to a contemplation of the mystery of the God the Father, the Son and the Holy Spirit. As we saw in Chapter 4 on the Hail Mary, this devotion leads us to contemplate what the Holy Trinity accomplished in Mary. The Father chose her and requested her consent to become the mother of Jesus; the Holy Spirit overshadowed her with his power; the Son of God became incarnate in her womb as her son and was born into this world as Our Lord Jesus Christ, our Saviour. As we say in the Hail Mary: *Blessed is the fruit of thy womb, Jesus.*

The Rosary enables us to gaze on the face of Jesus as we meditate on the mysteries of his life. Mary meditated on those mysteries throughout her life. We are told that she "treasured all these things and pondered them in her heart" (Luke 2:19). Mary pondered in her heart all that Jesus said and did. Those memories were always alive and active in her heart. As St Pope John Paul II wrote: "In a way those memories were to be the 'rosary' which she recited uninterruptedly throughout her life."[99] When we are praying the Rosary we are learning from Mary how to ponder the mysteries of Jesus her son and how to keep those mysteries alive in our hearts.

Once we begin to meditate on Mary's relationship with Jesus, we will automatically find ourselves meditating on the mysteries of the life of Jesus: the mysteries surrounding his conception, his birth and his childhood; the mysteries of his public life of preaching and teaching; the mysteries of his passion and death; the mysteries of his resurrection and ascension, and outpouring of the Holy Spirit.

That is why we say the Rosary is "a compendium of the Gospel".[100] These mysteries proclaim to us the good news of God's infinite love and mercy. As Jesus said, "God loved the world so much he gave his only Son, so that everyone may have eternal life. For God sent his Son into the world, not to condemn the world, but so that through him the world might be saved" (John 3:16-17). When we meditate on and pray the mysteries of the Rosary, we enter into every significant event in the life, death and resurrection of Jesus Christ. We begin to do what Jesus asks us to do when he says to us: "Make your home in me as I make mine in you" (John 15:4). We dwell in prayer on the mysteries of his life.

In the traditional Rosary we had a method, a model for contemplating Christ's life: his birth and childhood; his passion and death; and his resurrection and ascension into heaven. But we didn't have any specific mysteries that helped us to meditate on Jesus' public life of preaching the Gospel. Aware of this lacuna, St Pope John Paul II officially changed the order of the mysteries of the Rosary in 2002. He added a new set of mysteries, which he called the Mysteries of Light, or the Luminous Mysteries. Meditating on these mysteries enables us to accompany Jesus on his journeys as he went about preaching the Gospel.

Gazing on the Face of Jesus

While praying the Rosary we contemplate the face of Jesus Christ, with Mary and through the eyes of Mary. We learn from Mary to ponder in our hearts. She was Christ's first teacher and she also teaches us about her son, Jesus Christ. She was the first to gaze on the face of Jesus, the face of the Father's mercy. As Pope Francis, in his document calling for the Year of Mercy, wrote: "Jesus Christ is the face of the Father's mercy. These words might well sum up the mystery of the Christian faith. Mercy has become living and visible in Jesus of Nazareth, reaching its culmination in him."[101]

The great value of the Rosary as a prayer is found precisely in the way in which it enables us, through our meditation on the various mysteries, to keep our hearts and minds focused on Christ while at the same time acknowledging Mary's role as his mother and as our mother.

Mary was intimately involved in all the mysteries of the infancy and early life of Jesus. She was with him in his passion and at the foot of the cross when he died. She also experienced his glorious resurrection and ascension into heaven and the descent of the Holy Spirit on the apostles. The mysteries follow the proclamation of St Paul in his letter to the Philippians:

> Make your own the mind of Christ Jesus:
> Who, being in the form of God,
> did not count equality with God
> something to be grasped.
> But he emptied himself,
> taking the form of a slave,
> becoming as human beings are;
> and being in every way
> like a human being,
> he was humbler yet,
> even to accepting death,
> death on a cross.
> And for this God raised him high,
> and gave him the name
> which is above all other names;
> and so all beings
> in the heavens, on earth,
> in the underworld,
> should bend the knee at the name of Jesus
> and that every tongue should acknowledge
> Jesus Christ as Lord
> to the glory of God the Father.
> (Philippians 2:5-11)

The Creed as a Prayer

That great hymn of St Paul outlines how the Son of God became a human being like us, how he entered into the whole process of becoming human, how he humbly accepted death on the cross, and how God raised him to his right hand in glory through the resurrection. Praying the Rosary leads us systematically in a meditation on all these aspects of Christ's life. That is the real genius of the Rosary. Blessed Cardinal Newman, speaking about the Rosary, said:

> The great power of the Rosary lies in this, that it makes the Creed into a prayer; of course, the Creed is in some sense a prayer and a great act of homage to God; but the Rosary gives us the great truths of His life and death to meditate upon, and brings them nearer to our hearts.[102]

As a result of St Pope John Paul II's inspiration we now have twenty mysteries of the Rosary instead of the fifteen which the faithful have contemplated for many centuries. Just to remind ourselves, these mysteries are as follows:

The Joyful Mysteries

The Annunciation (Luke 1:26-38)

The Visitation (Luke 1:39-56)

The Nativity (Luke 2:1-20)

The Presentation in the Temple (Luke 2:22-40)

The Finding in the Temple (Luke 2:41-52)

The Mysteries of Light

The Baptism in the Jordan (Luke 3:21)

The Wedding at Cana (John 2:1-11)

The Proclamation of the Kingdom of God (Mark 1:15)

The Transfiguration (Luke 9:29-36)

The Institution of the Eucharist (Matthew 26:26-29)

The Sorrowful Mysteries

The Agony in the Garden (Luke 22:39-54)

The Scourging (Isaiah 53:1-5; John 19:1)

The Crowning with Thorns (Matthew 27:27-31)

The Carrying of the Cross (Luke 23:26-32)

The Crucifixion (John 19:17-37)

The Glorious Mysteries

The Resurrection (John 20)

The Ascension (Acts 1:1-11)

The Descent of the Holy Spirit (Acts 2:1-13)

The Assumption of Our Lady into Heaven

The Crowning of Our Lady in Heaven (Revelation 12)

These twenty mysteries enable us to contemplate the person of Christ, from the moment of his conception, through the power of the Holy Spirit, to the moment of his resurrection and return to sit at the right hand of God the Father in heaven. The whole prayer is very Christ-centred. As we say this pray we are accepting the invitation of Christ when he says to us: "Make your home in me, as I make mine in you" (John 15:4). As we pray the Rosary and meditate on the mysteries of Christ's life we begin to make our home in those mysteries. Jesus' whole life and mission pass through our minds and hearts as we ponder the mysteries of the Rosary. From the first moment of his conception in his mother's womb, through the power of the Holy Spirit, to the offering of himself for our salvation on the cross and his glorious resurrection from the dead and return to his Father in heaven, we contemplate the love of Jesus for us, as each of these mysteries unfolds in our hearts. That is why we say that although the Rosary is a great Marian prayer, it is first of all a great Christological prayer. In our meditation on each mystery, the whole focus is on Christ our Lord. As St Pope John Paul II said: "With the Rosary, the Christian people *sits at the school of Mary* and is led to contemplate the beauty of the face of Christ and to experience the depths of his love..."[103]

We pray each mystery in this way: we begin by saying the Lord's Prayer. This, as we saw in Chapter 3, is the prayer that Jesus taught us. We begin each decade of the Rosary with this great prayer to God our Father. We become aware that the Father is with us, that we are in his presence and that we are praying for the coming of his kingdom. Then we say ten Hail Marys (a decade) as we contemplate the love of the Father and the coming of the kingdom in some aspect of the life of Jesus. We conclude the decade with the Gloria. This "Glory be to the Father and to the Son and to the Holy Spirit" is a fitting response to the mystery of God's love contemplated in one of the mysteries of Jesus. The Joyful Mysteries are said on Mondays and Saturdays; the Sorrowful Mysteries on Tuesdays and Fridays; the Glorious Mysteries on Sundays and Wednesdays; and the Mysteries of Light on Thursdays.

We need about fifteen to twenty minutes to pray the Rosary. It is good to take our time. If you haven't got that length of time you could say just one or two decades. It is better to say one decade well than to rush the whole Rosary. As a method of prayer, the Rosary is at once vocal and contemplative, repetitive yet always changing.

The vocal side of the Rosary, saying the decade, is really the prelude to the contemplation: as we say the Hail Mary we are focusing on one of the mysteries of Christ's life. As the Methodist theologian Neville Ward wrote:

> It seems hard to believe that one can meditate on a theme while mentally repeating certain prayers even though these are so thoroughly known that little effort is required. As one becomes familiar with the Rosary the prayers gradually recede to form a kind of "background music", and the mystery is before the mind as though one is looking at a religious picture or icon. The balance frequently changes, and the prayers occupy the foreground of the mind for a time, and this may lead to a form of simple attention to God which is more like contemplation. If one finds one's mind being led into a stillness and concentration of this kind it is good to let it happen.[104]

The Manifestation of God the Father's Love

Many Protestants and Anglicans are rediscovering today, as Neville Ward did, that the Rosary opens up before our minds the whole panoramic view of the life and work of Jesus. As we contemplate each mystery we are gazing, as Ward said, at "a religious picture or icon". We now have twenty mysteries, twenty icons, of the life and work of Jesus to ponder as we pray the Rosary. Jesus sets the scene of our contemplation of each of the mysteries of the Rosary with these words: "God loved the world so much that he gave his only Son, so that everyone who believes in him may not be lost but may have eternal life" (John 3:16). Jesus makes it clear to us that the events of his life and mission on which we meditate, and which we call "the mysteries of the Rosary", are all manifestations of the Father's great love for us and the great mercy that he has shown to us. That is why we want to "make our home" in those mysteries of love.

The Distractions

We begin our Rosary with the good intention of contemplating the face of Christ in the mysteries of his life. Those mysteries are the focus of our hearts and minds as we say our Hail Marys. But while our hearts may be at rest in the mysteries, our minds, our thoughts can be all over the world. We become distracted. Instead of being focused on the mystery of the annunciation, or of the descent of the Holy Spirit, our minds can be preoccupied with the football results, or with some job that has to be done about the house, or with thinking about the weekend. These distractions can cause us a lot of unhappiness and we might even be tempted to give up on the Rosary. Some people will even say, "What's the point? I can never keep my mind on a mystery even for a few seconds, let alone for a full minute." It is important to remember, as we saw in Chapter 2, that we can turn our very distractions into moments of real contemplation. It is our thoughts, not the desire in our hearts for our time with God, that are easily distracted. But our hearts remain where we want to be. In our time of prayer we want to be with God, at home with Christ, at home in the mysteries of his life. We don't allow the distractions to convince us that we cannot pray or that we are wasting our time trying to pray. God sees our heart and he sees the good intention in our heart to pray the Rosary.

Need for Patience

We have to be patient with ourselves while praying the Rosary. We have the good intention to spend the time in God's presence. That intention is planted in our hearts by the Holy Spirit. All prayer begins with the desire to pray, and that desire always comes from God. Other desires in our hearts, however, always clamour for attention. Many of these desires are yearnings for things that are not always necessary for our well-being. We need a purification of these desires. God, in his loving care of us, purifies our desires when we enter into his presence in our prayer time. This purification of our desires takes place as we persevere with our prayer, despite all our struggles and apparent failures. As we alternate between contemplating the mysteries of the Rosary and concentrating on the words of the Hail Mary, we will struggle to keep our minds fully focused on what we are doing. But when we become aware that our thoughts are someplace else, we gently bring them back and remind ourselves that as we say the Hail Mary we are greeting Mary with the very same words the angel used: "Hail, full of grace, the Lord is with you." We are also pondering in some way the mystery of Mary becoming the Mother of God: the mystery of the Holy Spirit coming upon her and the birth of her Son and his early years growing up in Nazareth; we are pondering the mystery of Jesus preaching the Gospel, the Good News he brought to us from God; we spend time contemplating his suffering in his passion and death; we give God glory as we meditate on his glorious resurrection. The whole drama of our salvation unfolds before us as we meditate on the mysteries of the Rosary.

Taking a Contemplative Glance

When we become aware that our thoughts are elsewhere, we don't conclude that we are wasting our time or that we cannot pray. Rather, we thank God for alerting us to our distractions and we humbly and consciously refocus our minds on the mystery. We remind ourselves that prayer is God's gift and that the very fact that we are trying to pray is a sign that we have the gift. We can take a contemplative glance at Jesus manifested in the mystery or at Mary, his Mother, and her involvement in the mystery. For instance, if I have almost finished the third decade of the Glorious Mysteries, *the Descent of the Holy Spirit*, and I realise that my thoughts were elsewhere, I pause for a few moments, thank God for realising my distractions, take a contemplative glance at the coming of the Spirit on the apostles, and allow that awareness of the mystery to fill my thoughts and heart. I then conclude the decade with a grateful *Glory be to the Father and to the Son and to the Holy Spirit* in thanksgiving to God for the grace of becoming aware of the distractions and the grace of the contemplative glance at the Lord. I then proceed to pray the fourth decade and resist the temptation to pray the third decade once again because of all the distractions.

It is very important for us to remember that prayer is always a gift of God. Becoming aware of distractions is a great grace of the Holy Spirit. We can begin to see that the awareness of our distractions is a special grace of the Holy Spirit inviting us to look with a fresh gaze at the mystery that we are contemplating. And we remember the words of St Paul:

> The Spirit comes to help us in our weakness, for, when we do not know how to pray properly, then the Spirit personally makes our petitions for us in groans that cannot be put into words; and he who can see into all hearts knows what the Spirit means because the prayers that the Spirit makes for God's holy people are always in accordance with the mind of God. (Romans 8:26-27)

The Holy Spirit is with us as we pray the Rosary. When we are struggling with distractions the Spirit continues to pray our Rosary in us and for us.

Announce the Mysteries

It can be helpful, even while saying the Rosary alone, to clearly announce to yourself each mystery. For instance, you say, *The first Joyful Mystery: the annunciation.* Then take a brief moment to fix your mind on that scene: the archangel Gabriel is sent by God to ask the Virgin Mary to consent to become the mother of the Son of God. You now have a mental icon of the annunciation. If you are saying the Mysteries of Light, you announce to yourself, *The first Mystery of Light: Jesus is baptised at the Jordan.* Again, pause just slightly before you begin saying this decade and picture the scene: Jesus joins the crowds who are flocking to John the Baptist for baptism with water and, as he is at prayer, the Holy Spirit comes upon him and the voice from heaven says, "You are my Son; today have I fathered you" (Luke 3:22). Now you have a mental icon of the baptism of the Lord. As you say your decade your thoughts will probably fly off somewhere else, but once you become aware of these distractions, you gently refocus on the mystery, look again at the mental icon that you formed in your mind and continue peacefully with your prayer.

Making Our Home in the Mystery

No matter how much we have to struggle to keep our minds focused, we always take courage from knowing that while we are saying the Rosary we are accepting Jesus' invitation to make our home in his word and to live by his word. He said, "If you make my word your home, you will indeed be my disciples, you will learn the truth and the truth will set you free" (John 8:31-32). Praying the Rosary opens the door of Christ's home for us. Jesus invites us to enter into his home. In fact, he says to us, "Make your home in me as I make mine in you" (John 15:4). Jesus invites us to share and explore the mysteries of his life with him. The Rosary provides us, as we have seen, with a systematic way of embarking on this exploration. We enter into a deeply personal relationship with Jesus. That personal relationship with Jesus is the very essence of our Christian faith. Our Christian faith is not a whole series of doctrines or ethical norms. It is first and foremost our personal relationship with Jesus, our friendship with Jesus. We relate to him as we relate to our best friends. We trust him. The more we contemplate or meditate on the mysteries of his life, the more we get to know him. It is the very person of Christ whom we encounter as we make our home in the mysteries of the Rosary.[105] While praying the Rosary, we are free to move around in this "home of the mysteries" of Christ. Sometimes we are talking to God the Father; at other times we are talking to Mary, the mother of Jesus; throughout the prayer, by meditating on

Jesus' love for and obedience to his Father, we are absorbing the ethos of the mysteries of Christ.

Making our spiritual home in Christ's word, in his mysteries, fosters a deep Christian spirituality within us:

- a Trinitarian spirituality, acknowledging the Father, the Son and the Holy Spirit;

- a Christocentric spirituality, as we contemplate the mysteries of Christ's life, death and resurrection;

- a Marian spirituality, as we seek to see the mysteries of Christ through the eyes of his mother Mary.

In the Rosary, with Mary and through the eyes of Mary, we contemplate the face of Christ. Mary was the first to experience the mystery of her son and to ponder that mystery in her heart. We learn from her the secret of "pondering in our hearts", of keeping God's word in our hearts, of making our "spiritual home" in the mysteries of her son's life and teaching.

Saying the Rosary is never an escape from the trials and struggles of our daily life. We bring our whole life, all our concerns and hopes, to the Rosary. If you are facing some problem or difficulty, you can place it at the very centre of the mystery of the Rosary. My mother, who said the fifteen decades of the Rosary each day in her later years, was once deeply hurt by something a close friend said to her. When I phoned her to ask her how she was coping, she said, "It is gone now, but it took two Rosaries to get rid of it." She brought the hurt to the Rosary, and as she contemplated Christ in his great love and in all his suffering, her own hurt was healed.

The daily or regular praying of the Rosary forms within the mind the habit of contemplating Christ, keeps the mysteries of Christ at the forefront of our imagination and enables us to offer to God, in union with Christ, all our joys and sorrows. The Rosary is both a contemplative and a healing prayer. The mysteries of Christ become the focus of our contemplation. As we offer our whole life to God in the context of contemplating the mysteries of Jesus our Saviour, we experience peace and healing, forgiveness and reconciliation.

Many Catholics today are rediscovering for themselves the healing power of praying the Rosary. They find great peace in just lingering on the mysteries of Christ. Some Catholics who once had a great devotion to the Rosary, but who began to live their spiritual lives without it, are beginning to recognise that "making home in the mysteries of Christ" requires an interior discipline in prayer, and without the Rosary they find that more difficult. They are taking up once again the recitation of the Rosary and finding great grace and comfort in that time of prayer.

Blessed Pope Paul VI was a zealous advocate of the Rosary. He wrote: "The Rosary is an excellent prayer, but the faithful should feel serenely free in its regard. They should be drawn to its calm recitation by its intrinsic appeal."[106] We are not obliged to say the Rosary. It is not a sin not to say the Rosary. But of all the methods of prayer that have been developed and handed on from generation to generation in the Church over the past eight hundred years, there is none more effective or more enriching than the Rosary, our great Trinitarian, Christocentric and Marian prayer. It is our secure spiritual lifeline.

— Chapter 8 —

Praying for God's Mercy

Turning to God in prayer is never, in the first place, our initiative. It is always our response to God's invitation. He encourages us "to come to the throne of grace to receive mercy and find grace when we are in need of help" (Hebrews 4:16). St Alphonsus de Liguori personalises the "the throne of grace" in this way:

> The throne of grace is Jesus Christ, who is sitting on the right hand of the Father; not on the throne of justice, but of grace, to obtain pardon for us if we fall into sin, and help to enable us to persevere if we are enjoying his friendship. To this throne we must always have recourse with confidence; that is to say, with the trust which springs from faith in the goodness and truth of God, who has promised to hear those who pray to him with confidence, but with a confidence that is both sure and stable.[107]

It is to the person of Jesus that we come when we pray for God's mercy. We experience this prayer for God's mercy every time we celebrate the Holy Mass. At the beginning of Mass, just after we have acknowledged that we are sinners, in need of God's mercy, we appeal three times for mercy. We pray, or sing, *Lord have mercy, Christ have mercy, Lord have mercy.* Then as we say the beautiful prayer of praise, the Gloria, we pray, *Lamb of God, Son of the Father, you take away the sins of the world, have mercy on us; you take away the sins of the world, receive our prayer; you are seated at the right hand of the Father, have mercy on us.* Six times, in two prayers at the beginning of Mass, we appeal to the Lord for his mercy. And then, just before Holy Communion, we pray three times again for mercy as we say, *Lamb of God, you take away the sins of the world, have mercy on us.* Our most frequent request for ourselves in prayer during Mass is for God's mercy.[108]

Our Expectations

When we ask God for mercy, what are we expecting? How do we understand or visualise "mercy"? Let us begin by looking at the roots of our word *mercy*. Those roots are, of course, in the books of the Bible that we call the Old Testament, the Hebrew Scriptures. We find in those books the most wonderful prayers for God's mercy. In the morning prayer of the Church each Friday we pray with these words from the Book of the Psalms:

> Have mercy on me, God, in your kindness,
> In your compassion blot out my offence.
> Wash me more and more from my guilt
> and cleanse me from my sin.
> (Psalm 51:1-2)

That long psalm (there are nineteen verses in it) pleads with God to show us his mercy and compassion, his great love and his goodness, by giving us "a pure heart" and putting "a steadfast spirit" in us. We don't ask God for his mercy so that we can remain just as we are. Every time we ask God for mercy we are asking for a big change in our lives; we are asking for a new heart; for a new spirit; for a big conversion. And God says to us in response:

> I shall pour clean water over you and you will be cleansed; I shall cleanse you of all your filth and all your foul idols. I shall give you a new heart, and put a new spirit in you; I shall remove the heart of stone from your bodies and give you a heart of flesh instead. I shall put my spirit in you...
> (Ezekiel 36:25-27)

When we ask God for his mercy we are professing our faith in the true God revealed in Jesus Christ as "the Father of mercies and the

God of all consolation" (2 Corinthians 1:3) and we are asking for the grace of a deeper conversion in our lives. St Pope John Paul II put it this way: "Authentic knowledge of the God of mercy, the God of tender love, is a constant and inexhaustible source of conversion, not only as a momentary interior act but also as a permanent attitude, as a state of mind."[109]

When we are willing and ready to receive God's mercy, God will give us a new heart, a new spirit and cleanse us from all our sins. Then we, in our turn, become "as merciful as our heavenly Father is merciful" (Luke 6:36). We begin to live, as St Pope John Paul II said, "in a state of being continually converted". When we pray to God for mercy we are also asking for the grace to show mercy to others, just as when we pray to God for forgiveness, in the Lord's Prayer, we are asking for the grace to forgive others.

Roots of Our Word Mercy

Our English word mercy is derived from a Hebrew word which means womb. Cardinal Kasper writes: "It is characteristic of the Old and the New Testament that it uses the expression *rachamim* for 'compassion' and, for that matter, also for 'mercy'. This word is derived from rechem, which means 'womb'."[110]

Compassion is, then, compared to "mother love". Christ's compassion reveals "the mother love of God" for his people. As the Catechism of the Catholic Church teaches: "God's parental tenderness can also be expressed by the image of motherhood, which emphasizes God's immanence, the intimacy between Creator and creature."[111]

The prophet Isaiah makes a direct connection between a mother's love and God's love: "Does a woman forget her baby at the breast, or fail to cherish the son of her womb? Yet even if these forget, I will never forget you" (Isaiah 49:15). The image of mother may speak to you more clearly about the love, the compassion and the tenderness of God. God uses this image to encourage us: "At her breast will her nurslings be carried and fondled in her lap. Like a son comforted by his mother will I comfort you" (Isaiah 66:12-13). And we read in the psalm, "Enough for me to keep my soul tranquil and quiet like a child in its mother's arms, as content as a child that has been weaned" (Psalm 131:2).

The other Hebrew word from which our word for mercy is derived is *hesed*, which means faithfulness. God is faithful to his covenant with his people, and forgives their sin. God is faithful to himself when he forgives us, faithful to every promise he has made to us. That is why we can approach the throne of grace without fear. When we sincerely ask God for mercy he immediately fulfils his promise: "I will give you a new heart and put my own Spirit in you."

Our word *mercy* also has a Latin root: *misericordia*. This word is composed of *cor*, which means "heart", and *miseri*, which means "the poor". To have mercy literally means to have a heart for the poor. God has a heart for us poor sinners and when we appeal to him for his mercy he responds with great joy. Jesus tells us that "there will be more rejoicing in heaven over one sinner repenting than over ninety-nine upright people who have no need of repentance" (Luke 15:7).

Nothing, then, gives God greater joy than for us to come to him for his mercy and compassion. No matter how sinful our life may have been, no matter how often we may have fallen into the same sins, God never tires of forgiving us when our hearts are contrite, and we should never tire of asking for his forgiveness.

The Name of God

Pope Francis gave his book on mercy the title *The Name of God is Mercy*. He wrote: "We can say that mercy is God's identity card. God of Mercy, merciful God. For me this is really the Lord's identity."[112] Pope Francis never tires of speaking to the Church and the world about the mercy of God, urging everyone to put their trust in God's infinite mercy. He writes:

Mercy will always be greater than any sin; no one can put a limit on the love of the all-forgiving God. Just by looking at him, just by raising our eyes from ourselves and our wounds, we leave an opening for the action of his grace. Jesus performs miracles with our sins.[113]

We need to take to heart this great truth that "mercy is greater than any sin" because one of the most subtle temptations of the devil is to whisper in our ear that because we are sinners we have lost the love of God and we are no longer precious in his sight. Jesus told us this wonderful parable about how God shows his mercy:

Two men went up to the Temple to pray, one a Pharisee and the other a tax collector. The Pharisee stood there and said this prayer to himself, "I thank you, God, that I am not grasping, unjust, adulterous like everyone else, and particularly that I am not like this tax collector here. I fast twice a week; I pay tithes on all I get." The tax collector stood at a distance away, not daring even to raise his eyes to heaven; but he beat his breast and said, "God be merciful to me, a sinner." This man, I tell you, went home again justified; the other did not. Everyone who raises himself up will be humbled, but anyone who humbles himself will be raised up. (Luke 18:10-14)

We do not stand before God trusting in our own merits or good works, we stand before him trusting unconditionally in his mercy for us poor sinners. The greatest saints always see themselves as the greatest sinners. To the day we die we depend entirely on God's mercy and loving kindness. We live in hope. St Paul writes, "For we must be content to hope that we will be saved – our salvation is not yet in sight, we should not have to be hoping for it if it were – but, as I say, we must hope to be saved since we are not saved yet – it is something we must wait for with patience" (Romans 8:24-25). As we wait for our salvation to be revealed with patience and confidence in God's love and mercy, we give great glory to God. St Alphonsus assures us:

> God is much pleased with our confidence in his mercy, because we then honour and exalt that infinite goodness which it was his object in creating us to manifest to the world… St Bernard writes that the Divine mercy is an inexhaustible fountain, that he who brings to it the largest vessel of confidence shall take from it the largest measure of gifts: Neither, O Lord, do you put the oil of mercy into any other vessel than that of confidence.[114]

When we turn to God in prayer we come with the confidence of a child who runs to his or her father for help. The child will never say, "I am not good enough for my father to love and help me." Yet at times we are tempted to say that of God our Father. We are tempted to believe that because we are sinners, our Father in heaven wants nothing more to do with us. This is the most destructive distortion of the truth that God reveals to us and the most horrible lie that the devil can whisper into our ear.

There is just one law of the spiritual life: *start again*. As we open our whole life to God's mercy we become new. God doesn't keep a record of our sins: "Come, let us talk this over, says the Lord. Though your sins are like scarlet they shall be white as snow; though they are red as crimson, they shall be like wool" (Isaiah 1:18). God never forgets us, but the moment we ask for his mercy he forgets all our sins. Like the tax collector in the parable, we "go home justified" (Luke 18:14).

The Mercy of God is Our Merit

We don't stand upright before God because of our good works. We are justified by the mercy of God, not by anything we do. St Bernard expressed this well with these powerful words: "For my part, what I lack of myself, I confidently take to myself from the compassionate heart of the Lord which flows with mercy... The mercy of the Lord is, then, my merit. I am never bereft of merit as long as he is not bereft of mercy."[115]

St Bernard was inspired by these words of St Paul: "What proves that God loves us is that Christ died for us while we were still sinners" (Romans 5:8). God meets us in our sinful state and in his great mercy he reconciles us with himself. Through his mercy we are, as Jesus says, "reborn of water and the Holy Spirit" (John 3:5). We have to allow this truth to sink into the core of our being: *God loves me, not because I am holy, but because he wants to share his love and holiness with me.* We can never deserve to be loved in that way. When we gratefully open our heart to receive the free gift of God's infinite love, our heart becomes new, our whole being in renewed.

God's love purifies us from all our sins and makes us holy in God's sight. Now we gratefully accept ourselves and, in the words of the psalm, we can say to God:

It was you who created my inmost self,
and put me together in my mother's womb;
for all these mysteries I thank you;
for the wonder of myself, for the wonder of all your works.
(Psalm 139:13-14)

God teaches us as individuals to thank him for "the wonder of myself". In doing so, we are thanking him for the wonder of his creation and of our redemption. We can surely say with St Bernard: *Thank you; your mercy is my merit.* Now I no longer hold on to the guilt of sins that the Lord has forgiven. And I no longer feel the need to condemn myself because I am a sinner. When Pope Francis was asked in an interview, "Who is Pope Francis?", he said, "I am a sinner whom the Lord regards." All our great saints were deeply aware that they were sinners, but this consciousness of sinfulness didn't depress them or make them reject themselves. Rather, it filled them with joy, because every day their trust was not in their own good works, but in Jesus Christ who had come to save them from their sins. They could praise God for "the wonder of themselves" because they believed with St Bernard that the mercy of God was their merit.

Pope Francis has this liberating word of encouragement for all of us:

> To become saints, only one thing is necessary: to accept the grace which the Father gives us in Jesus Christ. There, this grace changes our heart. We continue to be sinners for we are weak, but with this grace which makes us feel that the Lord is good, that the Lord is merciful, that the Lord waits for us, that the Lord pardons us, this immense grace that changes our heart.[116]

The Evangelist of Mercy

Mary, the Mother of Jesus, was the great evangelist of God's mercy. On the way to visit her cousin Elizabeth, she had deeply pondered the great mystery of her own pregnancy. She had conceived the Son of God in her womb through the power of the Holy Spirit. She said in response to Elizabeth's praise, "The Almighty works marvels for me, holy is his name. His mercy is from age to age to those who fear him" (Luke 1:49-50). And then, thinking about what God was doing for God's people, she said:

> He protects Israel his servant,
> remembering his mercy,
> The mercy promised to our fathers,
> to Abraham and his sons for ever.
> (Luke 1:54-55)

Her pregnancy was the act of God "remembering his mercy", the manifestation of the mercy of the Father for his people. That is why we see in Jesus the face of the Father's mercy and why the proclamation that Jesus Christ is our Redeemer must always be the proclamation of mercy. Some people may have an image of God which excludes his tenderness and compassion. That is why Pope Francis, in calling for the Church to celebrate a holy year of Divine Mercy, wrote with a sense of urgency:

> The time has come for the Church to take up the joyful call to mercy once more. It is time to return to the basics and to bear the weaknesses and the struggles of our brothers and sisters. Mercy is the force that reawakens us to new life and instils in us the courage to look to the future with hope.[117]

It is only trust in the unconditional mercy of God that can fill our hearts with that living hope which we all need in life.

Foundation of the Church

The Church is built on the mercy of God revealed to us in Christ. It is not built on human wisdom. As members of the Church, each of us takes our stand on the solid ground of the mercy of God for all sinners, and we bear witness to that mercy by the way we relate to others. When we pray to God for mercy for ourselves and for the whole human race, we are standing on a sure foundation. All our actions as Christians, the way we relate to others, the way we have a word of encouragement and a word of forgiveness for them, the way we seek to comfort and console them in their hour of grief or desolation, the way we always seek to offer whatever help we can, all these actions reveal the mercy of God. As Pope Francis says, nothing in the witness of the Church to the world can be lacking in mercy. He writes: "The Church's very credibility is seen in how she shows merciful and compassionate love. The Church has an endless desire to show mercy. Perhaps we have long since forgotten how to show mercy and live the way of mercy."[118]

That observation of Pope Francis, "Perhaps we have long since forgotten how to show mercy and live the way of mercy", is addressed to each of us. Before we apply it to others we have to take it to ourselves. It is very easy to slip into judging and condemning others. Our response to others, in every situation, should always be motivated by mercy and compassion. Jesus is very blunt and specific about this. He says:

> Do not judge and you will not be judged; because the judgements you give are the judgements you will get, and the standard you use will be the standard used for you. Why do you observe the splinter in your brother's eye and never notice the great log in your own? And how dare you say to your brother, "Let me take that splinter out of your eye", when, look, there is a great log in your own. Hypocrite! Take the log out of your own eye first, and then you will see clearly enough to take the splinter out of your brother's eye. (Matthew 7:1-5)

We follow the way of mercy by not judging others, not gossiping about others, not condemning others. I think we would all see the contradiction in asking God for his mercy while refusing to treat others with mercy. It would be like asking God to turn a blind eye to our own sins while we broadcast what we imagine are the sins of others to anyone who is willing to listen.

Oasis of Mercy

Pope Francis employs a very beautiful image of the Church, of our communities and parishes and of each of us individually, when he writes: "Wherever the Church is present, the mercy of the Father must be evident. In our parishes, communities, associations and movements, in a word, wherever there are Christians, everyone should find the oasis of mercy."[119]

There are no lakes or rivers in a desert. But the traveller sometimes comes across a beautiful fertile place, with a spring or well of beautiful, fresh water. That is called an oasis. It is a safe, refreshing and restful place. Our parishes and our communities should be like that. People should feel safe, at no risk of being judged harshly, once they have reached the Church or found themselves in your parish community. Indeed, Pope Francis says, in the presence of any Christian, a person should feel a merciful, non-judgemental acceptance. They have arrived at "an oasis". Christians who walk this way of mercy grow in all the other virtues as well. They begin to understand what Jesus means when he says, "In truth, I tell you, in so far as you did it to one of the least of these brothers of mine, you did it to me" (Matthew 25:40). It is only through putting the Lord's words into practice that we can begin to understand them. Then we experience their effects in our lives.

The Call to Mercy

From his long experience of human frailty, his own as well as that of the thousands of people who sought his help as a priest and bishop, Pope Francis has a very realistic awareness of our struggles to "be merciful as our heavenly Father is merciful" (Luke 6:36). He is aware that if the Church is going to spread the good news of God the Father's mercy throughout the world, she must first of all begin to live that mercy in every situation. Each of us has to begin with our own experience of God's mercy. St Pope John Paul II said, "We must personally experience this mercy if in turn we want to be capable of mercy."[120] Living in this awareness of our own experience of God's mercy is how we come to get to know the Lord. As Pope Francis says: "Only he who has been touched and caressed by the tenderness of his mercy really knows the Lord. For this reason I have often said that the place where my encounter with the mercy of Jesus takes place is my sin."[121]

We gratefully remember the times when the Lord visited us with his mercy and took away all our sins. Those were moments of deep encounter with God when we got to know the Lord Jesus in new and transforming ways. We knew him as "the Lamb of God who takes away the sins of the world". This knowledge is not just *informative*, telling us something new about the Lord, it is also *transformative*, bringing about in us a deeper conversion in our life and a deeper commitment to living our Christian life. Our gratitude to God for his great mercy to us is expressed as we offer mercy and forgiveness to others.

As we pray to God for his mercy we begin to build our spiritual lives on mercy. We can look on every situation with the eye of mercy, refusing to attribute evil intentions to anyone. Bad things happen in life. While we acknowledge that they are bad, and while we may have to seek justice, we do not condemn the perpetrators as evil. We remember the words of Jesus on the cross: "Father, forgive them; they do not know what they are doing" (Luke 23:34). They thought that they knew exactly what they were doing and why they had to crucify Jesus. Caiaphas, the high priest, had said to the chief priests and Pharisees: "You do not seem to have grasped the situation at all; you fail to see that it is to your advantage that one man should die for the people, rather than that the whole nation should perish" (John 11:49-50). They had the best of intentions in seeking to have Jesus put to death. Yet Jesus, who knew the heart of man and who "could tell what someone had within" (John 2:25), could see that the knowledge that they thought they had was really a deluding form of ignorance.

St Paul makes the same excuse as Jesus when he writes: "None of the rulers of the age recognised it; for if they had recognised it, they would not have crucified the Lord of glory" (1 Corinthians 2:8). Indeed, St Paul made the same allowance for himself when he was a persecutor of the first Christian community in Jerusalem. He was known as Saul before his conversion, and he was a great enemy of Christians. The book of the Acts of the Apostles records: "Saul then began doing great harm to the Church; he went from house to house arresting both men and women and sending them to prison" (Acts 8:3). But through the mercy of God, after Saul's encounter with the risen Jesus, the Church's greatest enemy became the greatest preacher of the Gospel. As St Paul, he wrote:

> I thank Christ Jesus our Lord, who has given me strength. By calling me into his service he has judged me trustworthy, even though I used to be a blasphemer. Mercy, however, was shown to me, because while I lacked faith I acted in ignorance; but the grace of our Lord filled me with faith and with the love that is in Christ Jesus.
> (1 Timothy 1:12-14)

St Paul believed that he was the greatest sinner. This realisation filled him not with shame, but with absolute trust and confidence in the mercy of God. He had the transforming experience of God's mercy on the road to Damascus when Christ appeared to him and spoke to him in a blinding light (see Acts 9). Paul never forgot that it was through the grace of that conversion that he became a believer in Christ. We too must remember that we are believers in Christ not because we are more intelligent or better than those who don't believe in him, but simply because Christ has given us the gift of faith and shown us his mercy.

There but for the Grace of God

We can never know the heart of those who sin against us. But we do know that without the grace of God we would not do the good things we try to do each day. And we do know, too, from our own experience, that without the grace of God in our lives we would be capable of far more serious sins than the sins someone may commit against us. When we see someone engaged in evil actions we remember the words attributed to St Philip Neri: "There but for the grace of God go I." It is not through our own strengths, our own virtues, that we avoid evil actions but solely through the grace of God. As St Paul said, "It is by grace that you have been saved, through faith; not by anything of your own, but by a gift from God; not by anything that you have done, so that nobody can claim the credit" (Ephesians 2:8-9). In God's presence we always remember that we are in need of God's forgiveness. That is why Jesus taught us to pray "forgive us our offences". Before we think of the offences others may have committed against us, we remind ourselves of our need for God's forgiveness. Then we can pray with all humility to God our Father, "Forgive us our trespasses as we forgive those who trespass against us". In the depths of human suffering, forgiveness of those who inflict suffering and mercy shown to those who hate are the clearest signs that the kingdom of God is among us. That is how we bear witness to Christ in this world. In response to the mob who shouted, "Crucify him, crucify him" (John 19:6), Jesus whispered a prayer in his agony: "Father forgive them" (Luke 23:34). That prayer of Jesus from the cross still reverberates around our world. We are still trying to live by that word and example of Jesus in our families, parishes and communities. As St Pope John Paul II said, "Merciful love is supremely indispensable between those who are closest to one another: between husbands and wives, between parents and children, between friends."[122]

The Apostolic Exhortation: the joy of love

Following the two Synods of Bishops that were devoted to discussing the challenges facing the Christian family in the world today, Pope Francis published his Apostolic Exhortation, "The Joy of Love". It is a very encouraging and long letter on the love and mercy of God as experienced in family life. It is a beautiful letter, and reading it slowly and absorbing its teaching is spiritually most enriching. When discussing the unconditional love of God, Francis wrote:

> At times we find it hard to make room for God's unconditional love in our pastoral activity. We put so many conditions on mercy that we empty it of its concrete meaning and real significance. That is the worst way of watering down the Gospel. It is true, for example, that mercy does not exclude justice and truth, but first and

foremost we have to say that mercy is the fullness of justice and the most radiant manifestation of God's truth.[123]

God's mercy is the fullness of his justice! We may place conditions on God's mercy, to mistakenly take into account false notions of the demands of his justice, but God keeps reminding us that his mercy, like his love, is unconditional. God never says, "I will love you for as long as you are good." God doesn't love us because we are good and worthy of his love. It is God's love and mercy that make us worthy of his love. St Pope John Paul II, commenting on the Parable of the Prodigal Son and the reception the son received from his father on his return, wrote: "It becomes more evident that love is transformed into mercy when it is necessary to go beyond the precise norm of justice – precise and often too narrow."[124]

In the parable, the father runs to embrace his returning son, without a word of disapproval, and calls for a party because "this son of mine was dead and has come back to life; he was lost and is found" (Luke 15:24). The prodigal had left his father, but the father had never abandoned his son. The father had remained faithful to his fatherhood and to his son. The father in the parable portrays the love of God the Father for his prodigal sons and daughters. God never withdraws his love and mercy from us. In Pope Francis's words, "his mercy is the fullness of his justice".

St Paul said, "The proof of God's own love for us is that Christ died for us while we were still sinners" (Romans 5:8). And because of Christ's redeeming love, we can say to God our Father during Mass: "We thank you for counting us worthy to be in your presence and to minister to you." We receive the mercy of God not because we are worthy but because God wants to make us worthy. God is our Father, and in our Father's eyes we will always be his beloved children. In our Church, then, nobody, no matter how badly he or she behaves, is beyond the reach of God's mercy. That is why Jesus says to us, "Be merciful as your heavenly Father is merciful" (Luke

6:36). God looks on our sinfulness with mercy and compassion, but we are tempted to look on the sinfulness of others with rejection and slander. As we remain in touch with the mercy we ourselves have received from Christ, we can overcome all these temptations and show that same mercy to everyone in our lives. It is not our mercy; it is the mercy we ourselves have received from God that we need to share with others.

Our biggest difficulty in really appreciating the nature of divine love and mercy is that we tend to make our own love or mercy the measure of God's. And because our love or mercy can be quite limited, we tend to think that God must place some limits on his love or mercy. That is why God says very clearly to us: "My thoughts are not your thoughts and your ways are not my ways... For the heavens are as high above the earth as my ways are above your ways, and my thoughts above your thoughts" (Isaiah 55:8-9). We can easily say that God's love, mercy and forgiveness are infinite. And then we begin to place limits. As Pope Francis said, "We place so many conditions on mercy that we empty it of its concrete meaning and real significance."[125] Unconditional, divine love can never be reduced to the measure of conditional human love, nor can infinite, divine mercy be reduced to the measure of finite human mercy.

Living in Hope

Because God's love and mercy are infinite and unconditional we never lose hope for the future. The resurrection of Jesus from the dead was God's response to the worst that human beings could do to him. Sinful human beings plotted the death of Jesus, but God raised him up on the third day. For St Peter that is the ground of all our hope. He wrote: "Blessed be God the Father of our Lord Jesus Christ, who in his great mercy has given us a new birth into a living hope through the resurrection of Jesus from the dead" (1 Peter 1:3). Despite appearances, evil never has the last word in this world. God has and will always have the last word and it will be a word of resurrection, of a new creation. As he says at the end of the last book of the Bible: "Look, I am making the whole of creation new" (Revelation 21:5). We can calmly face the future, no matter what human sinfulness may throw at us, because we have this living hope in our hearts, and because we can look at every situation, no matter how bad it may be, with the eye of mercy. That look of mercy inspires us to pray to God the Father to have mercy. Jesus asked St Faustina to say this prayer and to teach the Church to say it: *For the sake of His sorrowful Passion, have mercy on us and on the whole world.* This is our response, in face of evil: we implore God to have mercy, reminding him, as it were, that Christ died for the whole human race. When we pray "have mercy on the whole world" we are praying for every person, good or bad, in the history of our world, because Jesus died for every person ever born into this world.

The Church as a Field Hospital

Pope Francis is fond of using the image of a field hospital after battle to describe the Church. Those who are wounded on their life's journey should always find healing and nursing in this hospital. Mercy is the medicine that the Church dispenses in this hospital. The members of the Church – that is, all of us – are the doctors and nurses in this hospital. We have to be close to the wounded. Pope Francis says:

> The Church must accompany with attention and care the weakest of her children, who show signs of a wounded and troubled love, by restoring in them hope and confidence... Let us not forget that the Church's task is often like that of a field hospital.[126]

Those who suffer with "a wounded and troubled love" often live on the edge of despair, thinking and fearing that life has lost its meaning and purpose. The medicine of mercy can restore their hope and confidence. We must be willing ministers of this medicine. We must have a word of encouragement for each person no matter how desperate their situation may appear. It is never beyond the power of God to bring good out of any evil, no matter what the situation. As the archangel Gabriel said to Our Blessed Lady, "There is nothing impossible to God" (Luke 1:37). But a wounded person may need to hear that from you many times before he or she really begins to believe it. And the good news is that wounded people don't have to solve all their problems at once. All that they have to do is take the first step. Pope Francis encourages us with these words:

> By thinking that everything is black and white, we sometimes close off the way of grace and of growth, and discourage paths of sanctification which give glory to God. Let us remember that "a small step, in the midst of great human limitations, can be more pleasing to God than a life which appears outwardly in order, but moves through the day without confronting great difficulties".[127]

Pope Francis repeats this teaching at every opportunity. When he was commissioning over a thousand priests as Missionaries of Mercy, for the Holy Year of Mercy, he emphasised very strongly to us that "nobody is held to do the impossible". He was encouraging us to recognise the limits under which some people have to struggle and not expect them to perform as if those limits weren't there. Even the smallest step, taken with trust in God's mercy, ensures that the person is once again on the right road.

When we pray to God for his mercy, we are asking for the one grace that God most of all desires to give us. We remind ourselves that God has given us this desire to ask for the transforming blessing of his mercy even before we turn to him in prayer. And we should always thank God for his invitation "to come to the throne of grace to receive mercy and find grace when we are in need of help" (Hebrews 4:16).

✛

— Chapter 9 —

A Dialogue of Love and Friendship
with Our Lord

Jesus calls us his friends. He says to us: "I call you friends, because
I have made known to you everything that I have learnt from my
Father" (John 15:15). Friends talk to each other about everything
that is going on in their lives. There is nothing too insignificant for
true friends. Because Jesus is our friend as well as Our Lord and
Saviour, our prayer will always flow from this reservoir of friendship.
We talk with Jesus, in our own words, from our hearts. We have, of
course, our formal prayers that we have looked at throughout this
book, but the heart of all those prayers is the prayer of friendship.
We know Jesus, we rejoice in his friendship and we speak with him
from our hearts. That is the essence of good prayer.

In calling us his friends, Jesus reveals to us our deepest identity. Only
Jesus, the Son of God, can fully reveal to us our true identity. He
enables us to see our true selves with the eye of faith. We are Christ's
friends, his brothers and sisters, God the Father's sons and daughters.
Jesus keeps reminding us that we were created by God his Father, we
are made in God's image and likeness, and through our redemption
"we have been reborn of water and the Holy Spirit" (John 3:5). Jesus
Christ, by becoming a human being like us, became a brother to
every human being ever born into this world. He acknowledges us
as his brothers and sisters, as his friends, and he invites us to live in
friendship with him. As a true friend, he reveals to us the mystery
of his own life and he wants to share his life deeply with us. In
his great prayer to God the Father he said: "I want those you have
given me to be with me where I am, so that they may always see the
glory you have given me before the foundation of the world" (John
17:24). Jesus' one desire for us is that we will share eternal life with

him and with God his Father. He gave us this clear description of eternal life when he said: "Eternal life is this: to know you the only true God, and Jesus Christ whom you have sent" (John 17:3). We know God through the light of faith that Jesus gives us and through the revelation that he has brought to us. It is because of that light of faith that we can accept and believe his revelation of God to us.

The Indwelling of the Holy Trinity in Our Hearts

One truly amazing truth that Jesus reveals to us is this: "If anyone loves me he will keep my word and my Father will love him, and we shall come to him, and make our home in him" (John 14:23). Without this divine revelation we would never even begin to imagine that the all holy God, the creator of the whole universe, and his Son, Jesus Christ, would come and dwell in our hearts. On this word of Jesus we can now say that God our Father dwells in our hearts, that Jesus our Redeemer also dwells in our hearts and that the Holy Spirit whom Jesus sends to us from the God the Father also dwells in our hearts. This is the profound mystery of the indwelling of the Holy Trinity in our hearts. St Paul had to ask the Corinthians: "Didn't you realise that you are God's temple and that the Spirit of God was living in you?" (1 Corinthians 3:16).

We believe these extraordinary truths about the three divine persons of the Holy Trinity making their home in our hearts because Jesus Christ reveals them to us. When we allow these truths to surface in our conscious mind, we are in a state of prayer. And the more frequently we dwell on them and embrace them in our hearts, the more abundantly will Jesus fill our hearts with gratitude to God, a gratitude that will express itself in our own spontaneous prayer of the heart.

"Christian prayer has a Trinitarian shape."[128] The indwelling of the Holy Trinity in our hearts and in the heart of all creation is the foundation of all prayer. It is customary to begin all our prayers with the words, "In the name of the Father, the Son and the Holy Spirit", and we conclude many of our prayers with the words, "Glory be to the Father and to the Son and to the Holy Spirit". And from the revelation of Jesus we believe that these three divine persons dwell at the very core of our being, where they have made their home in us. This is the spiritual source of the vitality of our life of faith. Rooted in the mystery of the indwelling of the Holy Trinity in our hearts, we can face every challenge as we look to the future with hope and absolute trust in God. In a beautiful line, Pope Benedict XVI wrote: "The success of our lives is found in our participation in the Trinitarian life offered to us."[129]

Dialogue of Love

Through the gift of prayer we enter into the mystery of God himself, into the unfathomable ocean of his love. Prayer becomes a genuine dialogue of love. When we open our hearts in friendship with Jesus we begin our dialogue of love with him. We talk to him about everything that is going on in our lives: the joys and worries of family life; every decision that we have to make; every new venture we may be thinking of undertaking. And, of course, we talk with him too about all our struggles, our failures, our weakness and sinfulness, and we do this without embarrassment, believing that we are talking with our closest friend who fully understands us and who is always faithful and ready to help.

This dialogue of love, unlike our time for formal prayers, is unstructured and spontaneous. Good people have often said to me, "I don't give much time to prayer, but I talk to God a lot throughout the day." They feel that if they are not down on their knees saying their formal prayers they are not giving much time to prayer. They feel great relief when I point out to them that talking to God in their own words throughout the day is the great gift of prayer, the prayer of the mystic, who lives in the presence of God and who finds God in all things and in all situations. Indeed, the very purpose of our times of formal prayer is to create within us that awareness of God's presence with us and within us throughout the day.

This dialogue of love is your own personal conversation with Christ, and the more you engage in it, the more frequent it will become. You developed the other friendships in your life by talking with your friends, by giving them time, by sharing with them some of your joys and sorrows. In a similar way, the more you talk with Jesus about your life, the closer you become to him and the more you will find yourself in communion with God each day. You will become more aware of his presence in your life and more aware of his divine providence in the daily events of your life. Instead of saying things like, "I was very lucky," you will thank God for his care in that situation. As someone said, "There are no coincidences, there are just God incidences." Living the life of faith opens our eyes to see the hand of God in all the events of the day. That is why St Paul says to us, "Pray constantly; for all things give thanks" (1 Thessalonians 5:17-18).

The Spontaneity of Our Dialogue with Christ

You have, I am sure, often found yourself talking quite spontaneously to the Lord about something or some person in your life. That spontaneity was the gift of the Holy Spirit. We seek to develop that spontaneity in our relationship with God. One of our old Redemptorist brothers, some years ago, was pressed for time and had to get the chapel ready for a service. To add to his problems, he knocked a flowerpot over in the sanctuary and was heard shouting, "Lord, give me a break. Can't you see I am hard pressed to get the chapel ready?" That was good spontaneous prayer, revealing a deep personal relationship with Jesus. That holy brother carried on this kind of spontaneous dialogue with the Lord throughout the day. He believed that Jesus was with him in every situation and he had a word with the Lord about every situation. He lived in union with God each day.

God wills us to live in union with him, not just when we say our formal prayers or go to Mass, but at all times and in all places. God is as truly present with you when you are doing your shopping in the supermarket as he is when you are on your knees saying your prayers. God is absent from no circumstance of our life. In fact, it is in and through the ordinary daily events of our life that God comes to us. As St Pope John Paul II said in his encyclical *Faith and Reason*, "God comes to us in the things we know best and can verify most easily, the things of our everyday life, apart from which we cannot understand ourselves."[130] As we become aware of God's presence in "the things of our everyday life" we find ourselves engaging in our dialogue of love and friendship with Christ and with God our Father. This dialogue, like all other forms of prayer, is the gift and inspiration of the Holy Spirit. Those moments of communion with God, as you go about your daily work, are the soul of all true prayer. You are now finding God in all things, in all places, in all the circumstances of your life. You are consciously living in the presence of God. In those moments you have become a true contemplative, a mystic. Those moments may not last long but they assure you that God is with you. They sanctify your whole day and give you a new vision for your day. You are now living a holistic spirituality which embraces both your relationship with God and all the activities of your daily life.

A holistic spirituality finds God in the familiar events and patterns of our life: in all our relationships; in family and friends; and even in those who are not our friends but may have become our critics or enemies. That is why Jesus says to us, "Love your enemies and pray for those who persecute you; in this way you will be sons and daughters of your Father in heaven" (Matthew 5:44-45). This is the real challenge we have to face on our way to our heavenly homeland. The God whom we love and seek to serve in this world is present not only in our friends, but also in our foes. That is why Christ says to us, "Pray for those who persecute you," because if we don't pray for them we will not be able to acknowledge that God is with them. And then we will find it very difficult "to love our enemies" as Jesus asks us to do. But the experience of those who actually pray for their enemies is that although they may never again become friends, the enemy no longer has power to rob their hearts of peace. They can see their enemy and wish him or her peace.

Practical Steps

Each of us has the capacity for contemplation. We can look in wonder at beautiful things; we can be deeply moved by human joy or sorrow; we can be still and silent in the presence of loved ones. In each of these emotions the deepest reality we experience is the presence of God. But so often we haven't woken up to God's presence. It is easy to say that we believe in the mystery of the indwelling of the Holy Trinity in our hearts, but it is not so easy to allow that truth to influence the way we live and relate to others. We need a spiritual reawakening each day. So often our bodies are wide awake, taking part in all kinds of activities, but our spirits seem to be asleep, unaware of the divine life within. Yet, despite our forgetfulness, God is present within us – loving and sustaining us, and inviting us to a life of communion with Father, Son and Holy Spirit. God is present in each event and in each situation, but we need to wake up to his presence.

The poet and patriot Joseph Mary Plunkett, who was executed for his part in the 1916 Easter Rising in Dublin, was wide awake to God's presence, Christ's presence, in the world. His poem on this divine presence has been much appreciated:

> I see his blood upon the rose
> and in the stars the glory of his eyes,
> His body gleams amid eternal snows,
> his tears fall from the skies.
> I see his face in every flower;
> the thunder and the singing of the birds

are but his voice – and carven by his power
rocks are his written words.
All pathways by his feet are worn,
His strong heart stirs the ever-beating sea,
his crown of thorns is twined with every thorn,
his cross is every tree.

Plunkett saw in the ordinary things of this world a deeper reality. His contemplative spirit was awake to the presence of Christ in all things and in all people. But sometimes we may find it easier to rejoice in God's presence when we behold some beautiful scene than to see Christ really present in another person.

Our inner dialogue of love and friendship with Christ will begin to embrace everyone in our life when we ask the Lord to enable us to see all of them as he sees them. At times we may see some of them as an enemy, or a drunk, or a beggar, or a nuisance, but Christ sees his brother or sister in each of them. We need to "borrow" the eyes of Jesus to see them in the way he sees them. That is what our gift of faith is. It gives us a new vision of the world and of everyone God has placed in this world.

The Gift of Each New Day

If we want to grow in this spirituality of finding God in all things and of engaging in our dialogue of love and friendship with Christ about everything that is going on in our lives, we need to discipline our hearts and minds so that our spirits stay awake during the day. This is the importance of having some form of morning prayer. As we wake up to a new day, we should also wake up to the presence of God in the new day and thank him for the gift of the new day. This new day has never been here before. God has just created it for us. Many people who went to sleep the night before didn't wake up to welcome the new day. That is why the simple prayer *Thank you Lord for the gift of this new day* is so powerful and effective.

You may be saying that the morning is not your best time for any kind of prayer. But you don't have to make eloquent speeches to God. All you have to do is acknowledge his presence, thank him for the new day and offer him all your thoughts, words and actions of the day. It makes no difference if you are still half asleep. A sleepy offering to God will have the same effect on your spirit as a chirpy one!

A Dialogue with Jesus or with Our Inner Critic

Our dialogue of love and friendship with Christ that we have been talking about is not, of course, the only dialogue that goes on in our hearts. In fact, all day long we are engaged in some kind of dialogue. Sometimes in that dialogue we can be making a very critical self-assessment: finding fault with ourselves and sometimes saying things to and about ourselves that we would never tolerate if they came from someone else! We are responding to what the psychologists call "the inner critic" or "the pathological critic". This is an inner voice that always says something negative, never says a good word about you, and no matter how well you may be doing, will always find some grounds for criticising you. This "inner critic voice" is not to be confused with the voice of God, which always encourages us. Nor is it to be confused with the voice of conscience, which always points out the right thing to do, and if we do the wrong thing, always draws that to our attention. The inner critic voice is not about right or wrong but about how you failed to perform some task with excellence. It keeps repeating negative evaluations of how you have done, maybe even calling you stupid or comparing you unfavourably with someone in your family or some friend. It keeps repeating: "You should have done better"; "You never get anything right"; "You start but you never finish"; "You are never on time." No matter how well you do, the inner critic will never say, "Well done."

Engaging in dialogue with the inner critic is not only useless, because you will never get a word of encouragement from it, it is also very undermining of your self-esteem. God wants us to see ourselves as he sees us. Throughout the scriptures God assures us that we are made in his image and likeness, that we are precious in his sight, that we are "his work of art", that he loves us with an everlasting love and that he will never cease loving us. God wants us to believe his words and to live by his words. The inner critic wants the opposite. It wants to put us down and make us feel that we are not much good at anything. Because we have lived with our inner critic all our lives, psychologists point out that no matter how outrageous its attacks are, it is generally always believed. That is why many of us can find it hard to accept any word of praise. We always try to push the praise away by saying something like, "I could have done better."[131]

But we don't have to listen to the inner critic, nor do we have to respond to it. Instead, we need to immediately substitute our dialogue with Christ our Lord for the dialogue that the inner critic wants to engage in. Our dialogue with the word of God is life-affirming. Speaking about this dialoguing with the word of God, Pope Benedict wrote: "We were created in the word and we live in the word; we cannot understand ourselves unless we are open to this dialogue."[132]

Our daily interior dialogue can and should be with God, who created us, who dwells in our hearts and who is encouraging us to reach our full potential, which is holiness of life. When we are talking with Jesus about our struggles, our difficulties, our joys and our sorrows, the inner critic has to remain silent. In fact, as soon as our inner critic begins to sound off, we should immediately begin our dialogue with Jesus. We can say, for instance, *Lord, you know I tried to do my best. I failed, but with your help I will do better next time.* The inner critic has no answer to that.

We live by God's word, not by the word of the inner critic. In living our life of prayer, it is most important for each of us to be convinced of this truth and to do our best each day to silence the negative voice of the inner critic. Often good people say to me, "But perhaps that inner voice is speaking the truth." As I mentioned above, the voice of God speaks the truth and the voice of conscience speaks the truth, but the inner critic applies a norm of excellence that we can never attain. God wants us to attain holiness of life by his grace, and when we respond to his grace we are growing in holiness. We do not attain holiness by our own efforts. But many of us have been brought up on what a priest friend of mine loved to call "muscular Christianity" – the idea that it is all down to our own efforts.

Some years ago a very discouraged priest arrived at our Renewal Centre. I listened to his story on the first evening and discovered that the cause of his discouragement was the fact that he couldn't pray. All his parishioners were praising him for his zeal and good work, but because he himself was not praying he was beginning to feel an awful hypocrite and was heading for a nervous breakdown. His inner critic was tormenting him. When I heard his story I opened the Bible at Chapter 43 of the prophet Isaiah and asked him to read it out to me. This took him a bit by surprise, but he read out these familiar words:

> Do not be afraid, for I have redeemed you;
> I have called you by your name, you are mine.
> Should you pass through the sea, I will be with you;
> or through rivers, they will not swallow you up…
> Because you are precious in my eyes,
> because you are honoured and I love you…
> Do not be afraid, for I am with you…
> (Isaiah 43:1-2. 4-5)

When he had read this passage I said to him: "God has just spoken to you. Do you want to respond?" He was silent for a few minutes, pondering this in his heart, and then he said with considerable emphasis, "He is not speaking to me." He could not believe that God was telling him that he was precious in his eyes or that he was honoured and loved by God. He had no problem believing that every single person in his parish was precious in God's eyes, but he could not believe it of himself. He felt that God just about tolerated him. He believed that God came to others through his priestly ministry, but he had no sense of God coming to him himself. His inner critic had filled him with self-negativity. I suggested to him that he should attend the Holy Hour that evening and join the sabbatical group of around sixty priests and religious who were on our three-month renewal course. I said, "The only prayer I want you to say as you sit before the Blessed Sacrament is, *Jesus, I thank you that I am precious in your Father's eyes.*" He gave me a rather strange look but quickly said, "All right, I will give it try." And he did. He told me afterwards that during that first evening of trying to make the Holy Hour he would look around occasionally and see all the others absorbed in their prayer while he was sitting there wringing his hands and trying to mean what he was saying when he said, "Jesus, I thank you that I am precious in your Father's eyes." But he kept it up each evening and after about three days of making the Holy Hour with the group he was so full of prayer that he couldn't stop praying. He was spending hours in the church.

What had happened to him? He had silenced his inner critic that was filling him with negativity about himself and had begun his dialogue with Jesus. He stayed with us for a month. By the time he left he was completely renewed in his spirit. Gone was his daily dialogue with his inner critic and in its place was a life-affirming dialogue of love and friendship with Jesus and with God his Father. I have often reflected on his experience and on the power of the simple prayer, *Jesus, I thank you that I am precious in your Father's eyes.* It also made clear to me that the only way to silence the inner critic is to begin a new dialogue with the Lord, who says to us, "I call you my friends."

That priest went back to his parish full of confidence and with his heart full of prayer. Not only was he saying all the official prayers of the Church with joy and gratitude each day, his dialogue of love and friendship with the Lord continued throughout the day. He would suddenly find himself talking to the Lord, praising his name and thanking him for all his graces and blessings. St Thérèse described well the kind of prayer he was now experiencing: "For me, prayer is a surge of the heart; it is a simple look turned toward heaven, it is a cry of recognition and of love, embracing both trial and joy."[133]

The Surge of the Heart

This "surge of the heart" which he was now experiencing was the soul of all the other prayers he said during the day. As a priest he had to say many formal liturgical prayers in the celebration of the sacraments and in praying the Divine Office. Without that "surge in the heart", those prayers had remained very dry and at times tedious. But with the grace of his new dialogue of love and friendship with Jesus, with his new awareness that he was truly precious in the Father's eyes, those formal prayers came alive for him. He rejoiced when he was standing in God's presence at the altar and leading his parishioners in the great Eucharistic prayer of thanksgiving which is the Mass.

There comes a moment in all our lives when God wants to give us a new grace of prayer. St Paul said, "Pray all the time, asking for what you need, praying in the Spirit on every possible occasion" (Ephesians 6:18). We know that we cannot be on our knees all day, so how can we pray all the time? This is the great grace that Jesus encourages us to ask from God:

> Ask and it will be given to you; search and you will find; knock and the door will be opened to you... If you then, evil though you are, know how to give your children what is good, how much more will your heavenly Father give the Holy Spirit to those who ask him! (Luke 11:9, 13)

It is only through the gift of the Holy Spirit that we can pray, as St Paul says, "on every possible occasion".

As we saw in Chapter 2, it is in our hearts that we respond to the gift of prayer, and even when we are busy going about many things, our hearts can still be focused on God. Jesus says to us, "Set your hearts on his kingdom first, and on his righteousness, and all these other things will be given to you as well" (Matthew 6:33). If our hearts are focused on God, then that "surge of the heart" will happen and we will find ourselves engaged in an inner dialogue of love and friendship with Jesus at unexpected moments. We will become aware of being in God's presence. The more frequently we acknowledge his presence with us during the day, the more we will experience this spontaneous dialogue in our hearts. We will be speaking to God from our hearts, no longer depending on the formal prayers that we say at other times of the day.

The Need for a Spiritual Alarm Clock

St Alphonsus de Liguori used very practical means to alert himself to the presence of God. He kept a clock on his table which chimed every fifteen minutes. When he heard those chimes, Alphonsus opened himself more consciously to the presence of God and lived that moment more intensely believing that God was with him. His example was a great help to me one year. I was a student at our international house in Rome in 1966. On my corridor on the third floor, there was just one phone. If a student received a call he would have to come to that phone. It was outside my door. For the first day or two I didn't mind answering the phone and walking along the corridor to tell students they had a phone call. But after a few days I found I was beginning to resent it. Should I just ignore it, let it ring and wait for someone else to answer it? My resentment was beginning to turn into anger and unwillingness to be of help. Then I got the grace to remember St Alphonsus' clock. The phone could be my "spiritual alarm clock". I said to myself, *Each time that phone rings I will take it as a call from God to become aware of his presence.* From then on, the ring of the phone woke up my

163

slumbering spirit. As I walked to answer the phone I was able to have a conscious moment with God in prayer. In fact, that phone became the occasion of my best prayer during that year. Every time the phone rang I was able to "raise my mind and heart to God". For me, God was on the line. Then I could celebrate the sacrament of the present moment. It is in the present moment that God is truly present, and once we open our hearts to his presence we have a true encounter with God. We begin again our dialogue of love and friendship with the Lord. The "surge of the heart" happens.

As we come to the end of this book on prayer you might find it very helpful if you could identify for yourself one or two "spiritual alarm clocks" that would give you a wake-up call during the day. This will be a great help to you as you seek to live each day in the presence of God. As prayer is our spiritual lifeline with the Lord, the more we breathe in its spiritual oxygen, the more intimate our communion with God will become and the more frequent will be our dialogue of love and friendship with the Lord.

❖

— Notes —

1. Office of Readings, Friday of tenth week of Ordinary Time

2. Pope Benedict XVI, *Jesus of Nazareth: from the baptism in the Jordan to the Transfiguration* (London: Bloomsbury, 2007), 131

3. St Alphonsus Liguori, *Prayer: the great means of salvation and of perfection*, ed. Paul A. Boer, Sr (Veritatis Splendor Publications, 2012), 57

4. Ibid., 53

5. Catechism of the Catholic Church, 2599

6. Pope Benedict XVI, *Jesus of Nazareth: from the baptism in the Jordan to the Transfiguration* (London: Bloomsbury, 2007), 18

7. Pope Benedict XVI, *Sacramentum Caritatis*, 85

8. Pope Francis, *Evangelii Gaudium: the joy of the Gospel*, 1

9. Pope Benedict XVI, *Jesus of Nazareth: from the baptism in the Jordan to the Transfiguration*, (London: Bloomsbury, 2007), 311

10. Ibid., 132

11. In St Matthew's account of the Lord's Prayer, Jesus teaches us to say, "Our Father". It is St Matthew's account that we use in our own prayer and in the Church's public prayer in the Mass.

12. Pope Benedict XVI, *Deus Caritas Est: God is love*. In his second volume of *Jesus of Nazareth*, Pope Benedict devotes a great chapter to the High Priestly Prayer of Jesus at the Last Supper. I am greatly indebted to this wonderful study. I recommend it to everyone who wants to learn more about the person of Jesus and the prayer of Jesus.

13. Second Vatican Council, Constitution on the Church, 4

14. Second Vatican Council, Decree on Ecumenism, 1

15. St Augustine, *Confessions*, 10. 27

16. Divine Office of Readings, Wednesday of fifth week of Lent

17. Pope Francis, Homily, 2 November 2015

18. Wilfrid Harrington OP, *Our Merciful God* (Dublin: Dominican Publications, 2016), 14

19. Second Vatican Council, Constitution on the Church in the Modern World, 22

20. Ibid.

21. St Alphonsus Liguori, *Prayer: the great means of salvation and of perfection*, ed. Paul A. Boer, Sr (Veritatis Splendor Publications, 2012), 10

22. Ibid., 26

23. Catechism of the Catholic Church, 2728

24. Ibid., 2729

25. St Alphonsus Liguori, *Prayer: the great means of salvation and of perfection*, ed. Paul A. Boer, Sr (Veritatis Splendor Publications, 2012), 57

26. See Luke 11:2-4 for St Luke's version of the Lord's Prayer

27. Blaise Pascal, *Pensées* (Penguin Classics edition) (London: Penguin, 2003), 127

28. St Augustine, *Confessions*, 10. 27

29. Second Vatican Council, Constitution on the Church in the Modern World, 22

30. Pope Francis, Homily, 2 November 2015

31. Catechism of the Catholic Church, 239

32. Pope Benedict XVI, *Jesus Of Nazareth: from the baptism in the Jordan to the Transfiguration* (London: Bloomsbury, 2007), 135

33. St Augustine cited in the Catechism of the Catholic Church, 2794

34. Tertullian cited in ibid., 2814

35. St Pope John Paul II, *Redemptoris Missio: on the permanent validity of the Church's missionary mandate*, 7 December 1990, 18

36. Second Vatican Council, Constitution on the Church in the Modern World, 16

37. Catechism of the Catholic Church, 1849

38. Pope Benedict XVI, *Jesus of Nazareth: from the baptism in the Jordan to the Transfiguration* (London: Bloomsbury, 2007), 147

39. Catechism of the Catholic Church, 2763

40. Pope Benedict XVI, *Jesus of Nazareth: from the baptism in the Jordan to the Transfiguration*, vol. 1 (London: Bloomsbury, 2007), 154

41. Catechism of the Catholic Church, 2837

42. Ibid., 2846

43. The *New Jerome Biblical Commentary* (London: Geoffrey Chapman, 1990), 645

44. Second Vatican Council, Constitution on the Sacred Liturgy, 11

45. Pope Francis, *Evangelii Gaudium: the joy of the Gospel*, 285

46. Kallistos Ware, "The Mother of God in Orthodox Theology and Devotion", in *Mary's Place in Christian Dialogue: occasional papers of the Ecumenical Society of the Blessed Virgin Mary 1970-1980*, ed. A. Stacpoole (Slough: St Paul Publications, 1982), 180

47. Second Vatican Council, *Lumen Gentium: Constitution on the Church*, 62

48. St Pope John Paul II, *Mother of the Redeemer*, 47

49. Ignace de La Potterie, *Mary in the Mystery of the Covenant* (New York: Alba House, 1992), 18

50. St Pope John Paul II, *Redemptoris Mater* (Mother of the Redeemer), 8 (italics in original).

51. John McHugh, *The Mother of Jesus in the New Testament* (London: Darton, Longman and Todd, 1975), 65

52. Ignace de La Potterie, *Mary in the Mystery of the Covenant* (New York: Alba House, 1992), 35

53. For a more detailed reflection on *kecharitomene* and Mary's response, see my book *All Generations Will Call Me Blessed* (Redemptorist Publications, 2007), from which the above section is taken

54. Heinrich Denzinger and Adolf Schönmetzer, *Enchiridion Symbolorum* (Freiburg: Herder, 1963), art. 252

55. St Pope John Paul II, *Mother of the Redeemer*, 4

56. British Methodist Roman Catholic Committee, *Mary, Mother of the Lord: sign of grace, faith and holiness. Towards a shared understanding*, 1995, para 6

57. Christoph Cardinal Schönborn, *We Have Found Mercy* (San Francisco: Ignatius Press, 2012), 119

58. St Pope John Paul II, *Mother of the Redeemer*, 45

59. Second Vatican Council, Constitution on the Church in the Modern World, 7

60. Decree on Ecumenism, 2

61. Catechism of the Catholic Church, 1091

62. Ibid., 1092

63. Ignatius IV of Latakia, Third World Assembly of Churches, July 1968 and published in the Uppsala Report (Geneva, 1969), p. 298, cited in Rupert Shortt, *God is No Thing* (London: Hurst and Company, 2016), 67

64. Tom Smail, *The Giving Gift: the Holy Spirit in person* (London: Darton, Longman and Todd, 1994), 173

65. Ibid.

66. Second Vatican Council, Constitution on the Church in the Modern World, 12

67. St Pope John Paul II, *Redemptor Hominis*, 18

68. Pope Benedict XVI, *Sacramentum Caritatis*, 85

69. Blessed Pope Paul VI, *Evangelization in the Modern World*, 75

70. Pope Francis, *Evangelii Gaudium: the joy of the Gospel*, 119

71. St Pope John Paul II, *Redemptor Hominis* 18

72. Pope Francis, *Evangelii Gaudium: the joy of the Gospel*, 1

73. Second Vatican Council, Constitution on the Church in the Modern World, 31

74. St Pope John Paul II, Encyclical on the Eucharist, 20 (italics in original)

75. 2nd Eucharistic prayer

76. 3rd Eucharistic prayer

77. Catechism of the Catholic Church, 1108

78. Second Vatican Council, Constitution on the Sacred Liturgy, 11

79. Second Vatican Council, Constitution on the Sacred Liturgy, 48

80. For a fuller exposition of all these prayer movements, see my book, *Going to Mass: becoming the Eucharist we celebrate* (Chawton: Redemptorist Publications, 2015)

81. The priest can choose from different forms of the penitential rite.

82. Pope Benedict XVI, *Sacramentum Caritatis: the Eucharist as the source and summit of the Church's life and mission*, 44

83. Second Vatican Council, Constitution on Divine Revelation, 21

84. Alexander Schmemann, *The Eucharist: sacrament of the kingdom* (New York: St Vladimir's Seminary Press, 2000), 76

85. See Pope Benedict XVI, *Verbum Domini, Post-Synodal Exhortation on the Word of God, 2010*, para 16

86. Pope Francis, *Evangelii Gaudium: the joy of the Gospel*, 138

87. Ibid.

88. 2nd Eucharistic prayer

89. St Pope John Paul II, Encyclical on the Eucharist, 11 (italics in original).

90. There are many possible responses to the invitation *Let us proclaim the mystery of faith*. I have used just one of them

91. 3rd Eucharistic prayer

92. St Augustine cited in the Catechism of the Catholic Church, 1396

93. St Pope John Paul II, Encyclical on the Eucharist, 22 (italics in original)

94. St Pope Leo the Great, Sermon 12 on the Passion. Cited by Raniero Cantalamessa, *The Eucharist: our sanctification* (Collegeville, MN: Liturgical Press, 1995), 39

95. Quoted in James T. O'Connor, *The Hidden Manna: theology of the Eucharist* (San Francisco: Ignatius Press, 1988), 61

96. St Pope John Paul II, Encyclical on the Eucharist, 6

97. St Alphonsus Liguori, *Visits to the Most Blessed Sacrament and the Blessed Virgin Mary* (Liguori, MO: Liguori Publications), 5

98. St Pope John Paul II, Apostolic Letter on the Most Holy Rosary, 2002, 2

99. Ibid., 11

100. Ibid., 19

101. Pope Francis, *Misericordiae Vultus: Bull of Indiction of the Extraordinary Jubilee of Mercy*, 1

102. Sayings of Cardinal Newman (London: Burns & Oates, 2004), 44

103. St Pope John Paul II, Apostolic Letter on the Most Holy Rosary, 2002, 1

104. Neville Ward, *Five for Sorrow, Ten for Joy: a consideration of the Rosary* (London: Epworth Press, 1971), xii

105. For a fuller reflection on this aspect of the Rosary, see my book *At Home in the Mysteries of Christ: the grace of the Rosary* (Chawton: Redemptorist Publications, 2016)

106. Blessed Pope Paul VI, *To Honour Mary*, 55

107. St Alphonsus Liguori, *Prayer: the great means of salvation and of perfection*, ed. Paul A. Boer, Sr (Veritatis Splendor Publications, 2012), p. 53

108. It is customary to conclude each of the Prayers of the Faithful with this refrain: *Lord in your mercy hear our prayer*. The invocation of the mercy of God is even more frequent in the Eastern Rites of the Liturgy than it is in our Latin Rite

109. St Pope John Paul II, *Rich in Mercy*, 13

110. Cardinal Walter Kasper, *Mercy: the essence of the Gospel and the key to Christian life* (New York: Paulist Press, 2014), 42

111. Catechism of the Catholic Church, 239

112. Pope Francis, *The Name of God is Mercy* (London: Bluebird, 2016), 7

113. Ibid., 82

114. St Alphonsus Liguori, *Prayer: the great means of salvation and of perfection*, ed. Paul A. Boer, Sr (Veritatis Splendor Publications, 2012), 51, 53

115. Office of Readings, Wednesday, Week 3

116. Pope Francis, *The Church of Mercy* (London: Darton, Longman and Todd, 2014), 14

117. Pope Francis, *Misericordiae Vultus: Bull of Indiction of the Extraordinary Jubilee of Mercy*, 10

118. Ibid.

119. Ibid., 12

120. St Pope John Paul II, *Regina Coeli* address, 23 April 1995

121. Pope Francis, *The Name of God is Mercy* (London: Bluebird, 2016), 26

122. St Pope John Paul II, *Rich in Mercy*, 14

123. Pope Francis, *Amoris Laetitia: the joy of love*, 311

124. St Pope John Paul II, *Rich in Mercy*, 5

125. Pope Francis, *Amoris Laetitia: the joy of love*, 311

126. Ibid., 291

127. Ibid., 305

128. St Pope John Paul II, *At the Beginning of the New Millennium*, 32

129. Pope Benedict XVI, *Sacramentum Caritatis*, 94

130. St Pope John Paul II, *Faith and Reason*, 12

131. For a full exploration of how to develop good self-esteem by living by God's word and denying the inner critic, see my book *The Inside Job: a spirituality of true self-esteem* (Chawton: Redemptorist Publications, 2004)

132. Pope Benedict XVI, *Verbum Domini*, 22

133. Cited in Catechism of the Catholic Church, 2558

Fr Jim McManus C.Ss.R.
Celebrating 60 years of ministry

 Jim McManus was professed as a Redemptorist on 8 September 1957 and celebrates the Diamond Jubilee of his Profession on 8 September 2017. He was ordained a priest in 1964 and for the next three years he pursued further studies in Rome. After teaching moral theology for six years in the Redemptorist Seminary he established Hawkstone Hall as a Sabbatical Spiritual Renewal Centre in 1973. For forty years, through three-month renewal courses, Hawkstone offered the opportunity for deep spiritual renewal to thousands of priests and religious men and women from all over the world. During his early work in Hawkstone Hall he realised that there was a need for a ministry of prayer for the healing of the hurts and inner wounds that many good people carry deep in their hearts. This led him to write several books on the healing ministry, on developing a spirituality of true self-esteem and forgiveness, and on cultivating true devotion in one's spiritual life. He is currently based in the Redemptorist Spirituality Centre in Scotland, in Perth, where his main mission consists of preaching parish missions throughout Britain, directing retreats for priests and religious in different countries, and encouraging the development of the healing ministry in parish life.